Mastering Masculine Fury

A Practical Self-Help Guide for Men Struggling with Anger

By

Calvin M. Duncan

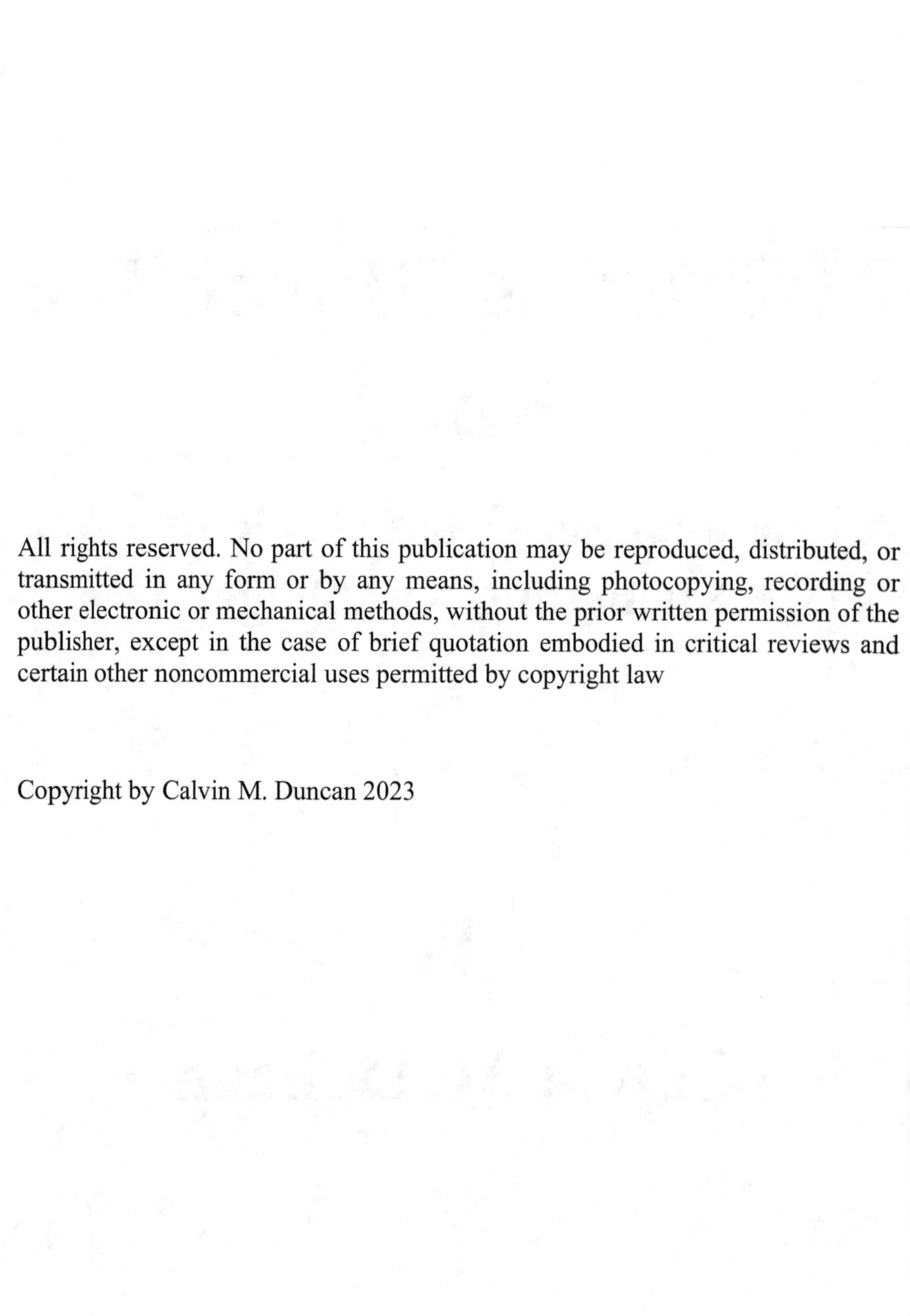

TABLE OF CONTENTS

- Emotional Regulation Exercises and Coping Strategies

- Building Resilience in Handling Life's Challenges

Chapter 7: Healing Wounds and Addressing Underlying Issues

- Exploring Past Trauma and Its Connection to Present Anger

- Therapeutic Approaches to Healing Emotional Wounds

- Addressing Underlying Issues for Long-Term Anger Management

Chapter 8: Sustaining Progress and Moving Forward

- Creating a Personalized Anger Management Plan

- Overcoming Relapses and Sustaining Progress

- Building a Support Network for Continued Growth

INTRODUCTION

Anger, an emotion that stirs within us like a tempestuous wave, is a universal human experience. It surges forth in response to perceived threats, injustices, or personal frustrations. For men, however, the landscape of anger often exists within a realm where societal expectations and traditional constructs of masculinity intersect with the expression of emotions.

Masculinity, as defined by cultural norms, has often mandated that men embody strength, control, and stoicism. Unfortunately, this construct has, at times, cast a shadow on the authentic expression and management of emotions, particularly when it comes to anger. Men are frequently urged to "tough it out," to suppress emotional responses, especially those deemed less acceptable or vulnerable. This suppression, however, can often lead to an internal pressure cooker, where emotions simmer and brew, waiting for an outlet.

The suppression of anger, whether due to societal expectations or personal internalization, does not eradicate its existence. Instead, it tends to linger beneath the surface, occasionally erupting in ways that surprise and even frighten. Unchecked, unmanaged anger can sabotage relationships, hinder personal growth, and manifest physically in stress-related ailments.

Understanding anger, especially in the context of masculinity, is crucial. This understanding does not imply the denial of anger or an attempt to eradicate it completely; rather, it advocates for its acknowledgment and, more importantly, its healthy management. It's about unraveling the complexity of this emotion and learning to navigate its currents, transforming it from a destructive force into a catalyst for personal growth and positive change.

In the following chapters, we'll embark on a journey that starts with understanding the roots of anger and its manifestations in the lives of men. We'll explore the intertwining of physiological responses and emotional triggers, investigating the mind-body connection in the realm of anger. From there, we'll delve into self-reflection, providing tools for men to assess their anger patterns and triggers, encouraging a deeper understanding of their own emotional landscape.

The heart of this journey lies in strategies for anger management. Cognitive-behavioral techniques, communication skills, and coping mechanisms will form the cornerstone of this section, offering practical tools for regulating emotions and responding to triggers in a more constructive manner.

Furthermore, the book addresses the impact of anger on relationships. Understanding how anger can affect personal connections—be it with partners, family members, or friends—will pave the way for strategies focused on resolving conflicts and rebuilding trust, crucial components for maintaining healthy relationships.

Stress management and emotional regulation are intertwined with anger management. Stress often acts as a catalyst for anger. Exploring stress management techniques, emotional regulation exercises, and lifestyle adjustments will provide a comprehensive approach to curbing the escalation of anger.

In acknowledging the complexity of emotions, this guide will also take a deeper dive into the relationship between past trauma and present anger. Addressing underlying issues through therapeutic approaches will offer a pathway to long-term healing and sustainable anger management.

The journey does not conclude with the mere understanding and management of anger; it extends to the sustainability of progress and personal growth. Building a personalized anger management plan, overcoming relapses, and establishing a support network are vital steps in moving forward on the path of emotional growth and stability.

This guide is more than just a manual; it's an invitation to embark on a transformative journey. It's a call to embrace the full spectrum of emotions, to break the barriers imposed by societal expectations, and to navigate anger with resilience and grace. It's about empowering men to master their emotions, fostering an environment where anger becomes a catalyst for personal evolution rather than destruction.

As we begin this exploration into the depths of anger and its management, it's essential to remember that acknowledging and addressing anger is not a sign of weakness. Instead, it's an act of courage and self-awareness. It's a commitment to personal growth, healthier relationships, and a more fulfilling life.

The journey of understanding anger in the context of masculinity is an invitation to reclaim emotional authenticity and find balance within the tempest of feelings. It's a journey that doesn't just lead to the management of anger; it leads to personal empowerment and a life lived with emotional intelligence.

CHAPTER ONE

Unpacking Anger: Recognizing Its Causes and Triggers

Anger, a universal human emotion, is a complex and multifaceted feeling that often emerges in response to various internal and external stimuli. It's an emotional reaction deeply embedded in the human psyche, triggered by perceptions of threat, injustice, frustration, or even a clash between expectations and reality. Unpacking the layers of anger, especially within the context of masculinity, is a crucial step in understanding its causes and triggers.

For men, societal norms and expectations play a significant role in shaping the way anger is perceived and expressed. Throughout history, the portrayal of men as stoic and resilient figures has often perpetuated the idea that expressing anger is more socially acceptable and is even encouraged as a symbol of strength. However, this projection of anger as a masculine trait overlooks the nuances of this complex emotion and the diverse ways it manifests in different individuals.

Recognizing the causes and triggers of anger involves delving into the depths of human experiences and emotions. The origins of anger can often be traced to a plethora of sources, both internal and external. Internally, it might stem from unmet expectations, feelings of powerlessness, fear, insecurity, or a clash between personal values and societal norms. External triggers could range from conflicts in relationships, work-related stress, societal injustices, or even traumatic experiences from the past.

The identification of anger's causes is not always straightforward. In many cases, the triggers for anger may be deeply embedded in subconscious thoughts or past experiences, making them harder to recognize and address. For men, societal pressure often adds another layer of complexity, creating barriers to acknowledging these triggers due to the perceived necessity to appear strong and in control.

Understanding the causes and triggers of anger involves a deep introspective journey. It necessitates a willingness to confront the uncomfortable, to sift through one's experiences, emotions, and thought patterns. This process might involve self-reflection, possibly through journaling, therapy, or candid conversations with trusted individuals. It's an invitation to peel back the layers of emotions, to recognize and confront what lies beneath the surface.

Moreover, anger might not always present itself overtly. Sometimes it takes the form of more subtle emotions or behaviors such as irritability, sarcasm, or withdrawal. Recognizing these

subtle signs is essential in identifying the underlying causes of anger before it escalates into a more explosive expression.

Men, conditioned by societal expectations, might often find it challenging to acknowledge the vulnerability associated with recognizing and addressing their anger triggers. Vulnerability, often misconstrued as a sign of weakness, is, in reality, a fundamental aspect of acknowledging and addressing one's emotional landscape. It is through vulnerability that one gains strength in understanding and managing emotions.

Recognizing the causes and triggers of anger is a deeply personal journey. It's about navigating the maze of emotions, understanding the intricate web of experiences, and acknowledging that anger, in its essence, is a natural response to various life circumstances. It's about accepting the diversity in human emotional responses, allowing for an authentic expression of feelings without the weight of societal expectations.

Addressing anger's causes and triggers doesn't imply eradicating the emotion entirely. Instead, it involves developing a nuanced understanding of it, recognizing the patterns, and learning to respond to it in a more constructive manner. This process paves the way for healthier emotional regulation and aids in transforming anger from a disruptive force into a catalyst for personal growth and understanding.

In the journey of unpacking anger, men are invited to navigate their emotional landscape, embracing the authenticity of their feelings without the limitations of societal expectations. It's a call to recognize the diverse triggers of anger, acknowledging the complexity of emotions, and embarking on a journey toward emotional intelligence and resilience.

This journey is not easy, nor is it swift. It's a gradual unraveling, a process of self-discovery that requires patience, self-compassion, and a willingness to confront the uncomfortable. It's an expedition into the depths of human emotion, aiming not to suppress or deny anger, but to understand and navigate it in a way that empowers personal growth and fosters healthier emotional responses.

In recognizing the causes and triggers of anger, men step into a realm of self-awareness and emotional regulation. It's an act of courage and strength to acknowledge the diverse triggers and complexities of this emotion, enabling a transformation from a reactive response to a more considered and controlled reaction.

Understanding anger's causes and triggers is not just a personal journey—it's a societal shift. It's an invitation to redefine masculinity by embracing a fuller, more authentic emotional range. It's about allowing men the freedom to express and manage their emotions without the weight of outdated societal expectations. This recognition is a catalyst for personal growth, healthier relationships, and a more balanced life.

As men embark on the journey of recognizing the causes and triggers of anger, it's important to remember that vulnerability and self-reflection are not signs of weakness; they are gateways to emotional resilience and growth. By embracing the complexities of anger, men can traverse the path toward understanding and managing emotions with authenticity and grace.

In conclusion, recognizing the causes and triggers of anger is the first step toward managing this emotion effectively. It's a journey that requires courage, self-reflection, and a willingness to challenge societal norms. By unpacking the layers of anger, men can navigate their emotional landscape with greater insight and find a more balanced, authentic expression of their feelings. This understanding not only empowers personal growth but also contributes to a more nuanced, authentic perception of masculinity in the broader societal context.

Societal Perceptions of Men and Anger: Breaking Stereotypes

Societal expectations and perceptions often wield a profound influence on how men experience, express, and manage their emotions, particularly the complex and volatile one—anger. The construct of masculinity, as portrayed by cultural norms and reinforced through generations, has assigned a particular framework for men's emotional expression, especially regarding anger.

From a young age, boys are often taught to embody traits typically associated with masculinity—strength, resilience, control, and a sense of stoicism. These attributes form the basis of the 'ideal man', where emotional restraint and the suppression of feelings, particularly vulnerability and sadness, are championed. Expressing anger, however, tends to find a more permissible ground in this construct.

Anger, thus, becomes a more 'acceptable' emotion for men to exhibit. It is often seen as a sign of power, assertion, and control—a sentiment bolstered by cultural depictions of masculinity in various mediums such as movies, literature, and societal narratives. As a result, men might feel a subconscious pressure to express anger rather than vulnerability, as if anger is the only emotion that truly aligns with the construct of 'being a man.'

However, this perception is limiting and problematic. It fosters a one-dimensional image of masculinity, one that fails to recognize the rich and diverse emotional spectrum that men, like any human being, possess. It is not the expression of anger itself that is concerning, but the imbalance—where anger is often the only emotion that is openly embraced, while other emotions are shunned or confined to the shadows.

This limitation creates a double-edged sword. On one side, it pushes men into the rigidity of emotional suppression, leading to a pressure cooker effect where emotions simmer beneath the surface, waiting for an outlet. On the other side, it inadvertently perpetuates the notion that anger is the only acceptable emotion for men to express when faced with a variety of life's challenges.

Moreover, societal norms often play a significant role in the way anger is tolerated or condemned in men. For example, an assertive, commanding male leader might be lauded for expressing anger in the workplace, perceived as exhibiting strength and control. In contrast, the same display of anger in a different context, such as within a familial or social setting, could be viewed negatively, labeled as aggression or lack of emotional control.

The narrative surrounding men and anger is not only about its acceptance or rejection; it also delves into the consequences that come with this societal construct. Men, feeling the pressure to conform to these expectations, might find themselves wrestling with a whirlwind of emotions. They may internalize a belief that expressing vulnerability or seeking help for emotional management is a sign of weakness or failure.

This pressure to conform to societal norms often results in a mask of strength and control, hiding the internal battles and emotional turbulence experienced by men. It creates a barrier to seeking help, whether through therapy, counseling, or even casual conversations, as acknowledging the need for support could challenge the rigid construct of masculinity they've been taught to embody.

The impact of these societal perceptions on men's mental health cannot be understated. Studies have shown that men are less likely to seek professional help for emotional issues, including anger management, compared to women. The stigma attached to being vulnerable or admitting struggles in managing emotions often inhibits men from seeking the support they need.

Conversely, challenging these stereotypes and dismantling the rigid framework of masculinity is vital. It involves redefining and expanding the boundaries of what it means to 'be a man'. It's about acknowledging and normalizing the diversity of emotional expressions within men, enabling them to navigate their emotional landscapes authentically.

Men expressing emotions other than anger should not be seen as a deviation from masculinity but as a celebration of their emotional authenticity. Vulnerability and emotional expression should be perceived not as weaknesses, but as strengths—signs of courage, self-awareness, and a commitment to personal growth and healthier relationships.

Educating society and reshaping the narrative surrounding men and emotions is pivotal. It necessitates a shift in the way masculinity is portrayed and perceived, where a man's emotional range is not confined to the shackles of anger but is expansive, complex, and authentic.

The transformation doesn't happen overnight. It requires a collective effort—challenging societal norms, reimagining the portrayal of men in media, and encouraging open discussions that normalize emotional expression in men. It involves providing platforms and support networks that foster a more nuanced understanding of masculinity, one that allows for emotional depth and vulnerability.

This shift is not just about liberating men from the constraints of societal expectations; it's also about creating a more empathetic and understanding society. A society that values emotional authenticity and acknowledges the diverse range of emotions that every individual, regardless of gender, experiences.

By breaking stereotypes and redefining the societal perceptions of men and anger, we pave the way for a more inclusive and emotionally intelligent world. It's a step toward not just empowering men to navigate their emotional landscapes authentically but also fostering healthier relationships and a more balanced society.

Challenging the societal constructs and perceptions surrounding men and anger is pivotal for promoting emotional authenticity and mental well-being. It's a journey that involves reshaping the narrative of masculinity, normalizing a diverse emotional spectrum, and providing a supportive environment that celebrates emotional expression in men. This transformation holds the potential not just to empower men but to create a more empathetic, inclusive, and understanding society for everyone.

Physical and Psychological Impact of Unmanaged Anger

Unmanaged anger, a potent and complex emotion, possesses the potential to wield a profound impact, both psychologically and physically, on individuals. When anger remains unchecked, it has the ability to shape behaviors, thoughts, and even the body's physiological responses, leading to a spectrum of consequences that can significantly affect an individual's well-being.

At its core, anger is a natural and often adaptive response to perceived threats or challenges. When managed effectively, anger can provide motivation, spur action, or alert an individual to potential problems. However, when unmanaged, anger turns into a destructive force, negatively influencing an individual's mental and physical health.

Psychologically, unmanaged anger can cause detrimental effects, leading to emotional distress, strained relationships, and compromised mental well-being. Continual outbursts of anger might create rifts in personal connections, causing strain in relationships with partners, family, and friends. It can lead to feelings of isolation, loneliness, and a sense of disconnect from the people around them.

Persistent anger can also contribute to the deterioration of mental health. It often fosters a sense of helplessness, leading to feelings of frustration, guilt, and shame for not being able to control these emotions effectively. Individuals grappling with unmanaged anger might spiral into patterns of negative thoughts and perceptions, ultimately leading to increased stress, anxiety, and even depression.

Furthermore, unmanaged anger has been linked to a variety of physical health issues. The constant activation of the body's stress response due to uncontrolled anger can have adverse effects on the body. Prolonged exposure to stress hormones, like cortisol and adrenaline, can lead to a range of health problems, including high blood pressure, heart disease, and weakened immune function.

The physiological effects of unmanaged anger are not limited to the heart and immune system. Continuous anger is also associated with gastrointestinal issues, including stomach ulcers and irritable bowel syndrome. The tension resulting from sustained anger can manifest in chronic muscle tension, leading to headaches, migraines, and even chronic pain conditions.

Sleep disturbances are another significant consequence of unmanaged anger. The emotional turbulence often interferes with the ability to relax and fall asleep, resulting in insomnia or disrupted sleep patterns. The lack of adequate rest further exacerbates emotional distress and negatively impacts an individual's overall health.

In addition to these immediate physical and psychological effects, the long-term consequences of unmanaged anger are profound. Chronic anger can contribute to a general sense of discomfort and discontent, leading to a diminished quality of life. It has the potential to interfere with an individual's ability to function optimally in various domains, including work, social interactions, and personal pursuits.

The impact of unmanaged anger is not just confined to the individual experiencing it; it often ripples through their immediate environment. Families, workplaces, and communities bear the brunt of unmanaged anger, experiencing the fallout through increased tension, conflict, and a pervasive sense of unease. The negativity resulting from unmanaged anger can create a toxic environment, affecting not just the individual but the collective emotional well-being of those around them.

This ripple effect is not confined to the present; it often transcends generations. Individuals who grapple with unmanaged anger might unknowingly pass down these patterns of behavior to their children or loved ones, perpetuating a cycle of emotional turbulence that stretches across familial ties.

Recognizing the vast scope of the impact of unmanaged anger is the first step in addressing its consequences. The recognition that uncontrolled anger doesn't just affect the individual but permeates into all facets of life is crucial in motivating individuals to seek help and make changes.

Managing anger effectively involves a multi-faceted approach. It encompasses a range of strategies designed to address the triggers, cope with emotional reactions, and build healthier mechanisms for emotional regulation. Techniques such as cognitive-behavioral therapy, mindfulness practices, and stress-reduction exercises are pivotal in equipping individuals with the tools to navigate and manage their anger effectively.

The importance of seeking support cannot be overstated. While recognizing the need for help might initially be challenging, reaching out to mental health professionals, therapists, or support groups can significantly aid in managing anger and its associated consequences. Creating a support network of friends, family, or peers who understand and empathize with these challenges can also provide a valuable source of encouragement and assistance.

Moreover, preventive measures play a vital role in managing anger. Engaging in regular physical exercise, practicing relaxation techniques such as meditation or deep breathing, and maintaining a healthy lifestyle are effective means to mitigate stress, thereby reducing the likelihood of anger outbursts.

Unmanaged anger has a profound impact, both psychologically and physically, on individuals and those around them. Its repercussions stretch across personal, social, and even generational boundaries. Recognizing and addressing the consequences of unmanaged anger is the first step in navigating its complexities.

Managing anger effectively involves a commitment to self-awareness, a willingness to seek support, and the implementation of strategies designed to regulate emotions in healthier ways. By addressing the underlying issues and seeking appropriate help, individuals can mitigate the damaging effects of unmanaged anger, paving the way for a more balanced and fulfilling life.

CHAPTER TWO

Exploring the Relationship Between Emotional State and Physical Response

Emotions are an intrinsic part of the human experience, shaping our perceptions, actions, and overall well-being. They are a complex interplay of psychological and physiological elements that influence our day-to-day lives. The connection between our emotional state and the body's physical responses is a profound and intricate relationship, influencing our health, behavior, and overall quality of life.

The Nature of Emotions

Emotions, often referred to as the language of the mind, encompass a wide spectrum of feelings—happiness, sadness, anger, fear, surprise, and disgust, to name a few. These emotions are multifaceted and dynamic, arising in response to internal and external stimuli. They are the product of cognitive evaluations, physiological responses, and behavioral expressions, forming the complex tapestry of human experience.

The human brain, particularly the limbic system, plays a pivotal role in processing emotions. Structures like the amygdala and hypothalamus are crucial in recognizing and responding to emotional stimuli. The amygdala, for instance, is central in processing emotional reactions and memory formation, while the hypothalamus governs the body's hormonal responses linked to emotions.

Emotional States and Physiological Responses

Emotional states are closely linked to the body's physiological responses. When experiencing emotions, the brain triggers a cascade of reactions within the body, leading to changes in heart rate, breathing patterns, hormonal secretion, and even alterations in the immune system.

For instance, fear or stress triggers the release of adrenaline and cortisol, commonly known as stress hormones. These hormones activate the 'fight or flight' response, leading to an increased heart rate, heightened alertness, and a surge in energy, preparing the body to respond to perceived

threats. This response is an evolutionary mechanism designed to enhance survival in the face of danger.

Conversely, feelings of happiness and contentment can stimulate the release of endorphins and dopamine, neurotransmitters associated with pleasure and reward. These chemicals foster relaxation, a sense of well-being, and can even alleviate pain, contributing to a more positive emotional state.

Moreover, emotions like anger or frustration can lead to increased muscle tension, raised blood pressure, and erratic breathing patterns. The cumulative effect of these physiological responses, when prolonged or frequent, can have significant impacts on an individual's physical health.

Impact on Health

The relationship between emotional states and physical responses extends to overall health. Prolonged exposure to stress or negative emotions can contribute to a variety of health issues, both immediate and long-term.

Chronic stress, often linked to the inability to regulate emotions effectively, can lead to a range of health problems. High levels of stress hormones, if sustained, can weaken the immune system, making individuals more susceptible to illnesses and infections. Additionally, chronic stress is a major contributor to cardiovascular issues, including high blood pressure, heart disease, and an increased risk of strokes.

The body's physiological responses to negative emotions can also have an impact on the digestive system. Stress and anxiety are often linked to gastrointestinal issues such as irritable bowel syndrome, ulcers, and other digestive disorders. The body's 'fight or flight' response can divert blood away from the digestive system, leading to disruptions in digestion and absorption of nutrients.

Moreover, persistent negative emotions are linked to sleep disturbances. The body's heightened state of arousal, brought about by stress or negative emotions, can interfere with the ability to relax and fall asleep. Insomnia or disrupted sleep patterns can further exacerbate emotional distress, creating a cycle of increased stress and disturbed sleep.

On the other hand, positive emotions have been associated with improved health outcomes. Studies have shown that a positive emotional state, including feelings of happiness and contentment, can lead to a stronger immune system, a healthier heart, and a lower risk of chronic diseases.

Behavioral Responses and Emotional States

Emotional states also play a significant role in shaping an individual's behavior. The physiological responses to emotions can influence decision-making, interpersonal interactions, and overall behavior.

For instance, an individual in a state of anger or frustration might exhibit impulsive behavior, making decisions driven by emotional reactions rather than rational thinking. Similarly, chronic stress might lead to irritability, affecting communication and relationships with others.

Conversely, positive emotional states often lead to more pro-social behavior. Individuals experiencing feelings of joy or contentment tend to display more empathy, generosity, and are more likely to engage in behaviors that benefit their overall well-being and that of others.

The impact of emotions on behavior is not limited to immediate responses; it can also influence long-term choices and lifestyle. Chronic stress or negative emotional states might lead individuals to adopt unhealthy coping mechanisms, such as overeating, substance abuse, or a sedentary lifestyle, all of which can have long-term consequences on health.

Emotional Regulation and Health

The ability to regulate emotions is vital in maintaining overall health and well-being. Emotional regulation involves the capacity to recognize, understand, and manage one's emotions effectively.

Studies have shown that individuals with better emotional regulation skills tend to have lower levels of stress and anxiety, healthier interpersonal relationships, and improved overall mental health. They are more likely to make rational decisions, exhibit more resilience in the face of challenges, and experience fewer health issues related to stress.

Techniques and strategies aimed at emotional regulation can significantly impact an individual's overall health. Practices such as mindfulness, meditation, cognitive-behavioral therapy, and relaxation exercises have shown to be effective in helping individuals manage their emotions better, leading to improved mental and physical health outcomes.

Individual Variations in Emotional Responses

The relationship between emotional states and physical responses is not uniform; it varies significantly among individuals. Each person's emotional response to a given situation is influenced by a variety of factors, including genetics, past experiences, social environment, and cultural influences.

For example, two individuals might react differently to the same stressful situation based on their past experiences and coping mechanisms. Similarly, cultural norms and societal expectations often shape the way emotions are expressed and managed, influencing an individual's emotional responses.

Individual variations also play a role in the way emotions are perceived and expressed. Some individuals might have a higher emotional reactivity, leading to stronger physical responses to emotional stimuli, while others might exhibit a more subdued reaction.

The Role of Gender in Emotional Responses

The influence of gender on emotional responses is a topic of interest. Studies have suggested that while there might not be inherent differences in the experience of emotions between men and women, societal norms often shape the expression of emotions differently based on gender.

Men, for instance, might be socialized to suppress or mask certain emotions, especially vulnerability or sadness, while exhibiting anger or aggression more openly. This socialization could contribute to varied emotional responses and physiological reactions based on societal expectations of emotional expression.

However, it's essential to note that these gender-related differences in emotional expression are not inherent but are often influenced by societal constructs and cultural norms, and individuals might exhibit a wide range of emotions irrespective of gender.

The Impact of Environment on Emotional States

The environment plays a significant role in shaping emotional responses. From the social context to the physical surroundings, the environment influences an individual's emotional state and subsequent physiological responses.

Social support and interpersonal relationships are crucial factors in modulating emotional responses. A supportive social network can buffer the impact of stress and negative emotions, while a lack of social connections can contribute to increased emotional distress.

Furthermore, physical surroundings, such as natural environments, urban settings, or workplace environments, can influence emotional states. Natural surroundings have been shown to have a positive impact on emotional well-being, reducing stress and promoting feelings of relaxation and well-being.

The Impact of Emotional Intelligence

Emotional intelligence, the ability to perceive, understand, and manage one's emotions effectively, plays a significant role in moderating the relationship between emotional states and physical responses.

Individuals with higher emotional intelligence tend to exhibit better emotional regulation skills, leading to reduced stress levels and healthier emotional responses. They are better equipped to recognize and manage their emotions, leading to improved overall health and well-being.

In conclusion, the relationship between emotional states and physical responses is intricate and multifaceted. Emotions, deeply ingrained in human experience, have a profound influence on the body's physiological reactions, health, behavior, and overall quality of life.

The impact of emotional states on physical responses spans a wide spectrum of health outcomes. Chronic stress and negative emotions are linked to a range of health issues, from cardiovascular problems to digestive disorders, while positive emotional states contribute to better overall health.

The ability to regulate emotions is vital in managing the impact of emotional responses on health and behavior. Techniques and strategies aimed at emotional regulation play a significant role in maintaining mental and physical well-being.

Understanding the interplay between emotional states and physical responses is crucial in fostering a more comprehensive approach to health and well-being. It involves recognizing the influence of emotions on the body's physiological reactions and implementing strategies to manage emotions effectively for improved health outcomes.

Emotional intelligence, social support, and a conducive environment play essential roles in moderating the impact of emotions on physical responses. The ability to recognize, understand, and manage emotions effectively is crucial in navigating the complex relationship between emotional states and physical responses for a healthier and more balanced life.

Stress, Hormones, and Anger: The Interplay

Stress is an intrinsic part of human life, serving as a natural response to various stimuli and challenges. The body's response to stress involves a complex interplay between hormones, the brain, and the nervous system. Stress can trigger a cascade of physiological reactions, including the release of hormones like adrenaline and cortisol, which play a significant role in the body's response to perceived threats. The relationship between stress, hormones, and anger is a complex and multifaceted one, often influencing an individual's emotional responses and overall well-being.

Stress is a response triggered by the body when faced with a perceived threat or challenge. The stress response, commonly known as the 'fight or flight' response, is an evolutionary mechanism designed to prepare the body to respond to potential danger. In situations of stress, the brain signals the release of stress hormones, activating the body's response to cope with the perceived threat.

Various triggers can lead to stress, including environmental factors, life events, work-related pressures, financial issues, and interpersonal conflicts. The body's response to stress is a highly individual experience, with individuals exhibiting varying levels of resilience and coping mechanisms.

The body's response to stress involves the release of hormones, primarily adrenaline and cortisol. These hormones are crucial in preparing the body for action and dealing with the perceived threat.

Adrenaline, also known as epinephrine, is released by the adrenal glands and acts as a rapid response hormone. It causes immediate physiological changes, such as increased heart rate, heightened alertness, and a surge in energy, preparing the body for quick action in response to stress.

Cortisol, often termed the 'stress hormone,' is released over a longer duration in response to stress. It plays a crucial role in regulating the body's metabolism, immune function, and the body's response to inflammation. Cortisol levels rise in response to stress, aiding in the body's energy mobilization and coping mechanisms.

Stress and the subsequent release of hormones like adrenaline and cortisol have a significant impact on emotional responses, particularly the emotion of anger. The body's stress response, when prolonged or intense, can influence an individual's emotional regulation, leading to heightened emotional states and, in some cases, triggering anger.

Prolonged exposure to stress and elevated levels of cortisol can have adverse effects on an individual's mental and emotional state. Chronically elevated cortisol levels are linked to increased feelings of anxiety, irritability, and, in some cases, aggressive behaviors.

The surge in adrenaline due to the stress response can also contribute to feelings of frustration and anger. While the adrenaline rush is designed to prepare the body for action, if not utilized or channeled effectively, it can result in feelings of restlessness, irritability, and heightened emotional states, often leading to anger.

Moreover, chronic stress and high levels of cortisol have been associated with increased emotional reactivity, affecting an individual's ability to regulate emotions effectively. This heightened emotional reactivity can lead to more frequent and intense anger responses, impacting an individual's overall emotional well-being.

Anger, as an emotional response, is associated with various physiological reactions within the body. When an individual experiences anger, the body often undergoes changes similar to those experienced during the stress response.

The body's reaction to anger includes an increase in heart rate, elevated blood pressure, and heightened muscle tension. These physiological changes mirror the body's response to stress, often leading to a feeling of arousal and readiness for action.

The release of stress hormones in response to anger contributes to these physiological changes. Elevated levels of adrenaline and cortisol, triggered by the stress response to anger, can have similar effects on the body as those experienced during stress, leading to increased heart rate, muscle tension, and heightened alertness.

Chronic stress and the subsequent emotional responses, including anger, can have detrimental effects on an individual's overall well-being. Prolonged exposure to stress and high levels of stress hormones, such as cortisol, can lead to changes in the brain's structure and function, affecting emotional regulation and exacerbating anger responses.

Chronic stress can lead to alterations in the brain's limbic system, particularly the amygdala, which plays a pivotal role in emotional processing. Changes in the amygdala's structure can influence an individual's emotional responses, making them more susceptible to heightened emotional reactivity and difficulties in regulating emotions effectively.

Moreover, chronic stress often leads to a reduced threshold for emotional responses, leading to more frequent and intense anger outbursts. The cumulative effect of chronic stress on the body's hormonal responses can contribute to a vicious cycle of heightened emotional states, leading to more stress and increased feelings of anger.

The ability to regulate emotions effectively plays a crucial role in managing the impact of stress on anger responses. Techniques and strategies aimed at emotional regulation are pivotal in coping with stress and reducing the intensity and frequency of anger responses.

Mindfulness practices, such as meditation and deep breathing exercises, are effective in modulating the body's stress response and aiding in emotional regulation. These practices promote a sense of relaxation and calm, reducing the impact of stress on emotional reactivity.

Cognitive-behavioral techniques focus on identifying and challenging negative thought patterns associated with stress and anger, aiding individuals in managing emotional responses effectively. These techniques help individuals reframe their thoughts and responses to stress, leading to better emotional regulation and reduced anger responses.

Therapeutic interventions, including counseling and therapy, are also beneficial in managing stress and anger. These interventions provide individuals with the tools and coping mechanisms to address stressors effectively and develop healthier emotional responses.

Effective stress management techniques play a significant role in mitigating the impact of stress on anger responses. Individuals can adopt various coping mechanisms to manage stress effectively, thereby reducing the likelihood of heightened emotional states and anger responses.

Physical exercise is an effective stress management tool, promoting the release of endorphins, neurotransmitters associated with feelings of well-being. Exercise aids in reducing stress levels and enhancing emotional regulation, ultimately reducing the impact of stress on anger responses.

Relaxation techniques, such as yoga, progressive muscle relaxation, and guided imagery, contribute to stress reduction and emotional regulation. These techniques foster a sense of calm and relaxation, reducing the body's physiological response to stress and, subsequently, anger.

Healthy lifestyle choices, including maintaining a balanced diet, adequate sleep, and avoiding substances like alcohol and tobacco, play a crucial role in stress management. A healthy lifestyle promotes overall well-being, aiding in reducing stress and managing emotional responses effectively.

Social support and interpersonal relationships play a pivotal role in managing stress and emotional responses. Having a supportive network of family, friends, or peers can buffer the impact of stress on emotional well-being, reducing the likelihood of heightened anger responses.

Open communication and social connections provide individuals with a platform to express their emotions and seek assistance in coping with stress. Sharing feelings and experiences with others often alleviates emotional distress and aids in managing anger responses effectively.

Moreover, strong social support systems often serve as a source of comfort and guidance during stressful situations, reducing the intensity of the stress response and aiding in regulating emotions effectively.

The relationship between stress, hormones, and anger is a complex interplay with significant implications for an individual's emotional well-being. Stress triggers the release of hormones like adrenaline and cortisol, influencing emotional responses, particularly feelings of anger.

Chronic stress and high levels of stress hormones have detrimental effects on emotional regulation, exacerbating anger responses and impacting an individual's overall well-being. The

body's physiological responses to anger mirror those experienced during the stress response, often leading to heightened emotional states and increased arousal.

Emotional regulation, coping mechanisms, and social support play crucial roles in managing the impact of stress on anger responses. Techniques aimed at emotional regulation, stress management, and fostering social connections are effective in reducing the intensity and frequency of anger responses.

Understanding the intricate relationship between stress, hormones, and anger is pivotal in adopting strategies to manage emotional responses effectively. By addressing stressors, developing healthy coping mechanisms, and fostering social connections, individuals can navigate the complex interplay between stress, hormones, and anger for improved emotional well-being.

Mindfulness and Relaxation Techniques for Anger Regulation

Mindfulness and relaxation techniques offer valuable strategies to regulate and manage anger effectively. By fostering self-awareness and providing tools to navigate emotional responses, these techniques empower individuals to cope with anger in a healthier, more balanced manner.

Mindfulness as a Tool for Anger Regulation

Mindfulness is a practice centered around present-moment awareness and non-judgmental acceptance of one's thoughts, feelings, and surroundings. Mindfulness-based techniques, such as meditation and mindfulness exercises, offer individuals the opportunity to observe their emotions and reactions without being consumed by them.

Mindfulness provides individuals with the ability to recognize the early signs of anger, such as physical tension or changes in breathing. By acknowledging these signs, individuals can intervene before the escalation of anger. Mindfulness encourages individuals to observe their emotional responses without immediate reactions, promoting a more reflective and measured approach to managing anger.

Mindfulness Meditation for Anger Regulation

Mindfulness meditation is a specific technique that involves focusing on breath, bodily sensations, or a specific focal point while maintaining non-judgmental awareness. The practice of meditation offers individuals a space to explore their emotional landscape, allowing them to observe and acknowledge their anger without immediately reacting to it.

During mindfulness meditation, individuals learn to notice anger rising without identifying with it. The focus shifts to observing anger as a passing emotional state rather than an integral part of their identity. By nurturing this awareness, individuals can create a gap between the emotional response and their subsequent actions, leading to better regulation and management of anger.

Breathing Techniques and Mindful Relaxation

Focused breathing exercises are another aspect of mindfulness that aids in managing anger. Techniques such as deep diaphragmatic breathing or square breathing encourage individuals to regulate their breath, promoting a sense of calm and relaxation.

When individuals experience anger, their breath often becomes shallow and erratic. Mindful breathing techniques offer a way to reset this response. By consciously engaging in controlled, deep breathing, individuals can reduce physical tension and stress, ultimately aiding in the regulation of anger.

The Role of Acceptance in Mindfulness Practices

Acceptance is a fundamental aspect of mindfulness. It involves acknowledging and accepting one's emotional state without judgment. When individuals encounter anger, practicing acceptance allows them to acknowledge their feelings without condemning themselves for experiencing them.

By accepting their emotional state, individuals create a space for self-compassion, fostering a more empathetic and understanding approach toward their own feelings. This self-compassion aids in managing anger effectively, promoting a more balanced emotional response.

Mindfulness-Based Cognitive Behavioral Techniques for Anger

Mindfulness-based cognitive behavioral techniques (MBCT) combine elements of mindfulness practices with cognitive-behavioral therapy (CBT). MBCT focuses on recognizing and reframing

negative thought patterns associated with anger. The practice involves identifying triggers, challenging negative thoughts, and replacing them with more balanced and realistic perspectives.

Through MBCT, individuals learn to identify the underlying thought processes that contribute to their anger. By challenging and reframing these thoughts, individuals develop a more adaptive response to anger triggers, leading to better emotional regulation.

Relaxation Techniques for Anger Management

Relaxation techniques offer another avenue for managing and regulating anger. These techniques focus on promoting a sense of relaxation and reducing physical and emotional tension, aiding individuals in mitigating the impact of anger.

Progressive muscle relaxation involves systematically tensing and relaxing different muscle groups in the body. By consciously relaxing these muscle groups, individuals experience a reduction in physical tension, which is often associated with anger responses.

Guided imagery techniques encourage individuals to visualize calm and serene scenes, promoting a sense of relaxation. By focusing on pleasant and tranquil imagery, individuals are able to shift their attention away from anger triggers, facilitating a more serene emotional state.

Mindfulness in Daily Life

Incorporating mindfulness practices into daily life can aid in managing anger. Everyday activities, such as mindful eating, walking, or even chores, can serve as opportunities to practice present-moment awareness. By bringing attention to these daily tasks, individuals cultivate a sense of mindfulness, fostering a more conscious and deliberate approach to life.

Mindful communication is another aspect where mindfulness practices aid in regulating anger responses. By practicing attentive and non-reactive listening, individuals can engage in more empathetic and understanding communication, reducing the likelihood of escalating conflicts and anger.

Mindfulness-Based Stress Reduction Programs

Mindfulness-based stress reduction (MBSR) programs offer structured approaches to managing stress and emotional responses. These programs typically involve guided instruction in mindfulness practices, group discussions, and supportive environments aimed at fostering emotional regulation and stress management.

MBSR programs provide individuals with the opportunity to learn and practice mindfulness in a structured setting. Participants often report reduced stress levels, better emotional regulation, and a more balanced approach to managing anger following their engagement with these programs.

The Role of Practice and Consistency

Consistency and regular practice are crucial in reaping the benefits of mindfulness and relaxation techniques for anger regulation. Like any skill, the effectiveness of these techniques increases with regularity. By incorporating mindfulness into their routine and engaging in regular practice, individuals reinforce these strategies, leading to better emotional regulation over time.

The Significance of Seeking Professional Help

While mindfulness and relaxation techniques offer valuable tools for managing anger, individuals experiencing persistent and intense anger might benefit from seeking professional help. Therapists, counselors, or anger management specialists can provide tailored interventions and guidance to address more complex and chronic anger issues.

Professional interventions often combine various approaches, including cognitive-behavioral techniques, mindfulness-based therapies, and individualized strategies, to address an individual's unique anger triggers and responses effectively.

Mindfulness and relaxation techniques offer valuable tools for managing and regulating anger. By fostering self-awareness, promoting relaxation, and providing strategies to navigate emotional responses, these techniques empower individuals to cope with anger in a healthier, more balanced manner.

Mindfulness practices, including meditation, breathing techniques, and acceptance, aid individuals in recognizing and regulating anger responses effectively. Relaxation techniques, such as progressive muscle relaxation and guided imagery, contribute to reducing physical and emotional tension associated with anger.

Consistency and practice play a significant role in reaping the benefits of these techniques. By incorporating mindfulness into their routine and engaging in regular practice, individuals reinforce these strategies, leading to better emotional regulation over time.

While these techniques offer valuable tools for anger regulation, individuals experiencing persistent and intense anger might benefit from seeking professional help. Therapists, counselors, or anger management specialists can provide tailored interventions and guidance to address more complex and chronic anger issues.

Understanding and practicing mindfulness and relaxation techniques empower individuals to navigate anger response effectively, fostering a more balanced and healthier approach to emotional regulation.

CHAPTER THREE

Self-Assessment Tools for Understanding Personal Anger Patterns

Understanding personal anger patterns is crucial for effective anger management. Anger, a natural human emotion, can manifest in various forms, and its expression is unique to each individual. Self-assessment tools provide a structured approach to introspection, aiding individuals in recognizing, analyzing, and understanding their anger patterns. These tools offer valuable insights into triggers, reactions, and behavioral responses, empowering individuals to manage their anger effectively and develop healthier coping mechanisms.

Self-assessment in understanding personal anger patterns is pivotal in effective anger management. Self-awareness aids individuals in recognizing their emotional triggers, behavioral responses, and patterns associated with anger. It allows individuals to examine the root causes of their anger, aiding in the identification of specific triggers and underlying emotions linked to their anger responses.

Self-assessment tools offer a structured approach to introspection, encouraging individuals to explore their emotional landscape in a reflective and non-judgmental manner. By engaging in self-assessment, individuals can gain insights into their anger patterns, facilitating the development of more effective and tailored anger management strategies.

Common Self-Assessment Tools for Understanding Anger Patterns

Various self-assessment tools and techniques aid individuals in understanding their anger patterns. These tools encompass a range of approaches, from questionnaires and assessments to journaling and behavioral tracking.

Anger Journals

Anger journals involve maintaining a record of anger episodes, triggers, and subsequent responses. Individuals use journals to note down the situations that evoke anger, their emotional and physical responses, and the outcomes of their reactions. Over time, the journal provides a comprehensive view of recurring triggers, emotional responses, and behavioral patterns associated with anger.

Recording anger episodes in a journal encourages individuals to reflect on their emotional state, triggers, and responses. It aids in identifying recurring patterns, assisting individuals in recognizing trends or situations that consistently evoke anger. Reviewing these records fosters self-awareness and helps individuals anticipate and manage future anger responses more effectively.

Behavioral Tracking

Behavioral tracking involves monitoring and recording behavioral responses during anger episodes. Individuals track their reactions, including verbal responses, body language, and actions during moments of anger. Tracking these responses aids in recognizing maladaptive behaviors or patterns associated with anger.

By observing and recording their behavior during anger episodes, individuals can identify specific responses or actions that exacerbate the situation. This self-awareness enables individuals to focus on modifying and adjusting their behavioral reactions, fostering a more constructive approach to managing anger.

Questionnaires and Assessments

Psychometric questionnaires and assessments designed to evaluate anger patterns and responses are also valuable self-assessment tools. These tools typically consist of questions aimed at exploring an individual's emotional triggers, reactions, and the intensity of their anger responses.

These assessments provide individuals with a structured approach to introspection, encouraging them to reflect on their anger triggers, the intensity of their emotional responses, and the impact of their anger on their daily life. Results from these assessments help individuals gain insights into their anger patterns, allowing for a more focused and targeted approach to managing anger.

Online Resources and Apps

Online resources and smartphone applications offer a convenient platform for self-assessment and managing anger. These resources include questionnaires, tools, and guided exercises aimed at understanding and regulating anger patterns.

Many apps and online platforms offer mood tracking, journaling features, and guided exercises for anger management. These tools allow individuals to log their emotions, track anger triggers, and engage in exercises aimed at promoting relaxation and emotional regulation.

Identifying Triggers and Patterns

The primary goal of self-assessment tools is to aid individuals in identifying their anger triggers and patterns. Triggers can vary widely, from external events and stressors to internal thoughts or emotions. By recognizing these triggers, individuals can anticipate and prepare for situations that commonly evoke anger.

Common triggers might include stressful situations, conflicts, feelings of disrespect or unfairness, or even physical discomfort. Self-assessment tools assist in identifying specific triggers unique to an individual, aiding in the development of targeted strategies for managing anger responses.

Patterns associated with anger often manifest in behavioral responses, emotional reactions, and thought processes. Identifying patterns allows individuals to recognize maladaptive responses and develop more constructive coping mechanisms. Recognizing these patterns is pivotal in modifying responses and developing healthier ways to manage anger effectively.

Emotional Responses to Anger

Understanding the emotional responses linked to anger is an integral aspect of self-assessment. Anger can trigger a wide range of emotional responses, from frustration and annoyance to intense rage or resentment. Recognizing the spectrum of emotional reactions aids individuals in identifying the intensity and nuances of their anger.

Self-assessment tools assist individuals in exploring and categorizing their emotional responses during anger episodes. By recognizing these emotional states, individuals gain insights into the depth and intensity of their anger, enabling a more nuanced approach to managing and regulating these emotions.

Physical Manifestations of Anger

Physical responses to anger, often linked to the body's stress response, are also crucial aspects of self-assessment. Anger can manifest in physical symptoms, including increased heart rate, muscle tension, changes in breathing, and even headaches or digestive issues.

Monitoring physical responses aids individuals in recognizing the bodily signs associated with anger. Self-assessment tools assist in identifying these physical manifestations, aiding individuals in employing relaxation and stress reduction techniques to mitigate the physical effects of anger.

Cognitive and Behavioral Patterns

Cognitive and behavioral patterns associated with anger are key components of self-assessment. These patterns encompass thought processes, self-talk, and behavioral responses during moments of anger. Recognizing these patterns aids individuals in identifying maladaptive cognitive responses and developing more constructive thought processes.

Self-assessment tools encourage individuals to examine their thought patterns during anger episodes. By recognizing negative or exaggerated thoughts, individuals can reframe and challenge these patterns, leading to more constructive and balanced cognitive responses.

Developing Strategies for Anger Management

Self-assessment tools not only aid in recognizing anger patterns but also lay the groundwork for developing effective strategies for anger management. Understanding personal triggers, emotional responses, physical manifestations, and cognitive patterns guides individuals in tailoring and implementing targeted anger management techniques.

Cognitive Restructuring and Thought Modification

Cognitive restructuring involves identifying and challenging negative thought patterns associated with anger. Individuals utilize self-assessment insights to recognize and reframe maladaptive thoughts, promoting a more balanced and realistic perspective on anger triggers.

Thought modification techniques encourage individuals to replace negative or exaggerated thoughts with more constructive and balanced alternatives. By utilizing insights gained from self-assessment, individuals can adopt healthier cognitive responses to anger triggers.

Behavioral Modification and Coping Strategies

Behavioral modification strategies, rooted in self-assessment insights, focus on altering maladaptive behavioral patterns associated with anger. Individuals use self-awareness gained through self-assessment tools to recognize and modify responses during anger episodes.

Coping strategies, informed by self-assessment, offer individuals tools to manage anger effectively. Techniques such as deep breathing, relaxation exercises, and mindfulness practices aid individuals in regulating their emotional responses and mitigating the impact of anger triggers.

Effective Communication and Conflict Resolution

Recognizing triggers and patterns through self-assessment assists individuals in adopting effective communication strategies and conflict resolution techniques. Individuals use self-awareness gained from self-assessment to approach conflicts in a more constructive and balanced manner, fostering better communication and resolution.

Effective communication techniques, rooted in self-assessment insights, aid individuals in expressing their emotions and needs in a non-confrontational and assertive manner. Conflict resolution strategies aim to address conflicts constructively, leading to better outcomes and reduced triggers for anger.

The Role of Consistency and Ongoing Self-Assessment

Consistency and ongoing self-assessment are vital in effectively managing and regulating anger. Self-awareness gained through self-assessment needs regular reinforcement. Consistent self-reflection aids in tracking progress, identifying changes in patterns, and adapting strategies for more effective anger management.

Regular engagement in self-assessment techniques helps individuals recognize shifts in triggers, emotional responses, and behavioral patterns. By consistently assessing their anger patterns, individuals are better equipped to refine and adapt their strategies for managing and regulating their anger effectively.

Professional Guidance and Support

While self-assessment tools are invaluable for understanding personal anger patterns, individuals experiencing persistent and intense anger might benefit from seeking professional guidance. Therapists, counselors, or anger management specialists can provide tailored interventions, guidance, and support to address complex and chronic anger issues.

Professional interventions often combine various approaches, including cognitive-behavioral techniques, anger management strategies, and individualized counseling, to address an individual's unique anger triggers and responses effectively.

Conclusion

Self-assessment tools play a crucial role in understanding personal anger patterns, aiding individuals in recognizing triggers, emotional responses, behavioral patterns, and cognitive processes associated with anger. These tools offer valuable insights, empowering individuals to develop targeted strategies for managing and regulating their anger effectively.

By fostering self-awareness, self-assessment tools enable individuals to gain insights into their anger responses, empowering them to develop healthier coping mechanisms and more constructive approaches to managing anger. Consistency and ongoing self-reflection reinforce these insights, aiding in the adaptation and refinement of strategies for effective anger management.

While self-assessment tools provide valuable insights, individuals experiencing persistent and intense anger might benefit from seeking professional guidance. Therapists, counselors, or anger management specialists can offer tailored interventions and support to address more complex and chronic anger issues.

Identifying Anger Triggers and Behavioral Responses

Anger is a natural and complex emotion that can have both constructive and destructive effects. Identifying anger triggers and understanding behavioral responses to anger is crucial for effective anger management. This awareness allows individuals to recognize the factors that lead to anger and develop strategies for responding in a more balanced and constructive manner. In this exploration, we will delve into the nature of anger triggers and the various behavioral responses associated with anger.

Anger triggers are the events, situations, thoughts, or interactions that provoke feelings of anger. These triggers can vary widely from one person to another and may include both external and internal factors. Understanding and identifying anger triggers is the first step in managing anger effectively.

External Anger Triggers

External anger triggers are events or circumstances in the external environment that can provoke anger. These triggers are often related to interactions with others or external situations. Common external anger triggers include:

1. Conflict and Disagreements: Interpersonal conflicts, arguments, or disagreements with others can be potent anger triggers. When individuals perceive that their values, needs, or boundaries are not respected, anger may arise.

2. Injustice or Unfairness: Experiencing or witnessing unfair treatment, discrimination, or injustice can evoke strong feelings of anger. The sense of inequity and injustice can lead to anger as a response to perceived wrongdoing.

3. Rejection or Disapproval: Feelings of rejection, criticism, or disapproval by others can trigger anger, as these emotions may be perceived as a threat to one's self-esteem or social standing.

4. External Stressors: Stressful life events, such as financial difficulties, work pressures, or health issues, can trigger anger when individuals feel overwhelmed or unable to cope with the demands of their environment.

5. Physical Discomfort or Pain: Physical discomfort, illness, or pain can lead to heightened irritability and anger. Physical discomfort can make individuals more prone to experiencing anger due to their discomfort.

Internal Anger Triggers

Internal anger triggers are factors that originate within an individual's thoughts, emotions, or internal experiences. These triggers often involve perceptions, beliefs, or personal interpretations. Common internal anger triggers include:

1. Negative Thoughts: Negative thought patterns, self-criticism, or irrational beliefs can be internal triggers for anger. Catastrophic thinking or beliefs about the unfairness of life can contribute to anger.

2. Unmet Expectations: When individuals have unrealistic or unmet expectations, they may experience anger. Unfulfilled hopes or desires can lead to feelings of frustration and anger.

3. Emotional States: Negative emotions such as stress, anxiety, or sadness can trigger anger. Emotional states may be interconnected, and feelings of anger can emerge as a response to other negative emotions.

4. Past Trauma or Experiences: Unresolved past trauma or negative experiences can be internal triggers for anger. Past emotional wounds may resurface and provoke anger in response to similar situations or memories.

5. Low Frustration Tolerance: Some individuals have a low tolerance for frustration, making them more prone to experiencing anger when faced with minor setbacks or inconveniences.

Identifying and Recognizing Anger Triggers

Recognizing anger triggers requires self-awareness and introspection. It involves paying close attention to emotional responses and reflecting on the factors that lead to anger. Several strategies can help individuals identify their anger triggers:

1. Self-Reflection: Regular self-reflection allows individuals to examine their emotional responses and identify recurring patterns associated with anger. Journaling or keeping a diary of anger episodes can be a valuable tool for self-reflection.

2. Emotion Tracking: Tracking emotions and identifying when anger arises can provide insights into the triggers. Individuals can use apps or written logs to monitor their emotional states and the events that precede anger.

3. Therapeutic Support: Engaging in therapy or counseling with a trained professional can provide a safe and structured environment for exploring and identifying anger triggers. Therapists can offer guidance and insight into the underlying causes of anger.

4. Mindfulness Practices: Mindfulness techniques, such as meditation, promote present-moment awareness and self-reflection. These practices help individuals become more attuned to their emotional responses and the factors that trigger anger.

Understanding Behavioral Responses to Anger

Behavioral responses to anger encompass a wide range of actions, verbal expressions, and physical behaviors that individuals exhibit when they experience anger. These responses can vary significantly from person to person and can be either constructive or destructive.

Constructive Behavioral Responses to Anger

Constructive behavioral responses to anger are those that aim to address the underlying issues and promote resolution without causing harm to oneself or others. Constructive behaviors include:

1. Effective Communication: Engaging in open and assertive communication to express one's feelings and needs without resorting to aggression or blame. Constructive communication promotes understanding and conflict resolution.

2. Conflict Resolution Skills: Developing conflict resolution skills, such as active listening and negotiation, to address disagreements and conflicts in a respectful and productive manner.

3. Problem-Solving: Identifying the underlying issues that contribute to anger and working on problem-solving techniques to address the root causes of anger triggers.

4. Emotional Regulation: Employing relaxation techniques, mindfulness, and deep breathing to manage emotional responses and reduce the physiological arousal associated with anger.

5. Seeking Support: Recognizing when anger becomes overwhelming and seeking support from friends, family, or mental health professionals. Seeking help is a constructive response to anger, especially in cases of intense or chronic anger.

Destructive Behavioral Responses to Anger

Destructive behavioral responses to anger involve actions or expressions that harm oneself or others. These responses often exacerbate the situation and can lead to negative consequences. Destructive behaviors include:

1. Physical Aggression: Engaging in physical violence, including hitting, pushing, or other forms of physical harm toward others. Physical aggression is harmful and often illegal.

2. Verbal Aggression: Using harsh language, shouting, insulting, or verbally attacking others. Verbal aggression can damage relationships and escalate conflicts.

3. Passive-Aggressive Behavior: Behaving in a passive-aggressive manner by expressing anger indirectly, such as through sarcasm, sulking, or withholding communication. Passive-aggressive behaviors can lead to misunderstandings and increased tension.

4. Destruction of Property: Damaging or destroying property in a fit of anger, which can lead to legal consequences and financial burdens.

5. Self-Harm: Turning anger inward and engaging in self-harming behaviors, such as cutting or substance abuse. Self-harm is dangerous and requires immediate professional intervention.

Identifying Behavioral Responses to Anger

Identifying behavioral responses to anger involves recognizing one's actions and expressions during anger episodes. Individuals can use the following strategies to identify and understand their behavioral responses to anger:

1. Self-Observation: During moments of anger, individuals can engage in self-observation, paying close attention to their actions and words. This self-awareness aids in recognizing behavioral responses associated with anger.

2. Feedback from Others: Seeking feedback from friends, family, or trusted individuals can provide insights into one's behavioral responses to anger. Others may offer observations or feedback on how anger is expressed.

3. Recording Behaviors: Keeping a record or journal of anger episodes can help individuals track and identify their behavioral responses. Recording the sequence of events and actions during anger episodes offers valuable insights.

4. Therapeutic Intervention: Seeking professional guidance from therapists or counselors can aid in identifying and understanding behavioral responses to anger. Therapists provide a safe space for exploration and insight.

Developing Strategies for Managing Behavioral Responses to Anger

Developing strategies for managing behavioral responses to anger involves cultivating self-regulation, developing coping mechanisms, and fostering constructive ways to express and manage anger. Strategies for managing behavioral responses include:

1. Anger Management Techniques: Engaging in anger management programs that provide strategies for recognizing and managing behavioral responses to anger. These programs offer tools for self-regulation and emotional control.

2. Cognitive-Behavioral Therapy (CBT): CBT focuses on identifying and modifying negative thought patterns and behaviors associated with anger. It helps individuals develop more constructive and adaptive responses to anger triggers.

3. Stress Management Techniques: Employing stress reduction techniques, such as exercise, relaxation, and mindfulness, aids in reducing physiological arousal associated with anger, promoting calmer behavioral responses.

4. Conflict Resolution Training: Learning conflict resolution skills and effective communication techniques helps individuals address conflicts in a constructive and non-confrontational manner.

5. Social Support and Professional Help: Seeking support from friends, family, or mental health professionals offers guidance and assistance in managing and addressing behavioral responses to anger.

Understanding anger triggers and behavioral responses is essential for effective anger management. Anger triggers can be both internal and external factors that provoke feelings of anger, while behavioral responses encompass a wide range of actions and expressions exhibited during moments of anger.

Recognizing and identifying anger triggers involves self-awareness, introspection, and reflection. Self-assessment techniques and self-reflection aid in identifying triggers, allowing individuals to anticipate and manage their responses effectively.

Behavioral responses to anger can be either constructive or destructive. Constructive responses focus on resolution, effective communication, and emotional regulation. Destructive responses lead to harm and escalation of conflicts.

Identifying behavioral responses to anger requires self-observation, feedback from others, and record-keeping. Understanding these responses enables individuals to develop strategies for managing and regulating their behavior during moments of anger, promoting healthier and more constructive outcomes.

Developing effective strategies for managing anger triggers and behavioral responses involves engaging in anger management techniques, cognitive-behavioral therapy, stress reduction, conflict resolution training, and seeking support from friends, family, or professionals.

Journaling and Self-Reflection Exercises

Journaling and self-reflection exercises are powerful tools for personal growth, self-discovery, and emotional regulation. They provide a structured and accessible means of exploring one's thoughts, feelings, and experiences, including those related to anger. In this comprehensive exploration, we will delve into the significance of journaling and self-reflection exercises, their various forms, and how they can be harnessed to enhance emotional intelligence, manage anger, and improve overall well-being.

Journaling and self-reflection exercises have been utilized for centuries as valuable practices for self-exploration, understanding emotions, and fostering personal development. These techniques offer individuals a private space to express thoughts and feelings, uncover patterns, and gain insights into their emotional responses, including anger. By engaging in structured self-reflection, individuals can better understand their triggers, responses, and develop more constructive ways of managing their emotions.

The Power of Journaling

Journaling is the act of recording one's thoughts, emotions, and experiences in a written or digital format. It provides a space for self-expression, self-discovery, and personal growth. Journaling can be an effective means of exploring and understanding anger, as it offers several advantages:

1. Emotional Release: Journaling allows individuals to express and release pent-up emotions, providing a safe outlet for feelings of anger and frustration.

2. Self-Awareness: Writing about one's experiences and emotions fosters self-awareness. By putting thoughts and feelings into words, individuals gain clarity and insight into their emotional responses.

3. Identification of Triggers: Journaling helps individuals identify patterns and common triggers for anger. By examining past entries, individuals can uncover recurring themes and situations that evoke anger.

4. Anger Management: Through journaling, individuals can explore different strategies for managing anger, coping with difficult emotions, and improving emotional regulation.

5. Conflict Resolution: Journaling can assist in understanding conflicts and relationships. It enables individuals to reflect on their role in conflicts and develop insights into resolving interpersonal issues.

Forms of Journaling

Journaling can take various forms, each catering to individual preferences and needs. Here are some common types of journaling:

1. Emotional Journaling: This form focuses on exploring and understanding emotions, including anger. It involves recording one's emotional experiences, triggers, and the context in which anger arises.

2. Gratitude Journaling: Gratitude journals are dedicated to expressing thankfulness and positive emotions. While it may seem unrelated to anger, practicing gratitude can contribute to overall emotional well-being and reduce the likelihood of anger episodes.

3. Reflective Journaling: Reflective journals delve into personal experiences and their impact on emotions and thoughts. This form of journaling encourages self-reflection and introspection.

4. Dream Journaling: Dream journals involve recording dreams and analyzing their symbolism and emotional significance. This type of journaling can reveal subconscious emotions and stressors that may contribute to anger.

5. Bullet Journaling: Bullet journals are a structured form of journaling that uses bullet points, lists, and symbols to record thoughts, tasks, and goals. It's an effective way to keep track of triggers, emotional responses, and anger management goals.

Getting Started with Journaling

For those new to journaling, getting started can seem intimidating. However, it's a simple and flexible practice that can be tailored to individual preferences. Here are steps to begin a journaling practice:

1. Choose a Journal: Select a physical notebook or digital platform that suits your preferences. Some people prefer the tactile experience of writing by hand, while others opt for digital journaling apps for convenience.

2. Set a Schedule: Establish a regular journaling schedule. It can be daily, weekly, or as often as you feel the need to express and explore your emotions.

3. Find a Quiet Space: Choose a quiet and comfortable environment where you can concentrate on your thoughts and feelings without distractions.

4. Start with Prompts: If you're unsure how to begin, use journaling prompts. These are questions or statements that can kickstart your writing and encourage self-reflection. For example, "What triggered my anger today?" or "What are some healthy ways to manage my anger?"

5. Write Freely: There are no specific rules for journaling. Write freely and without judgment. Your journal is a safe space for self-expression, and there's no need to worry about grammar or structure.

6. Reflect on Past Entries: Periodically review your past journal entries. This allows you to identify patterns, changes, and progress in your emotional responses and anger management efforts.

7. Experiment with Different Forms: Try different forms of journaling to see which resonates most with you. You might find that emotional journaling is particularly helpful for understanding and managing your anger.

Self-Reflection Exercises

Self-reflection exercises complement journaling and provide individuals with additional tools for exploring their emotions and reactions, particularly those related to anger. These exercises encourage introspection, mindfulness, and personal growth.

1. The Five Whys

The "Five Whys" is a technique that encourages individuals to dig deeper into the root causes of their emotions, including anger. To practice the Five Whys:

- Start by identifying a recent instance of anger.

- Ask yourself, "Why did I feel angry in that situation?"

- After answering, ask "Why?" again in response to your initial answer. Continue this process five times, delving deeper into the underlying reasons for your anger.

This exercise helps individuals move beyond surface-level triggers and explore the core issues contributing to their emotional responses.

2. Daily Emotion Journal

In addition to regular journaling, consider creating a daily emotion journal. At the end of each day, record your primary emotions and any anger episodes you experienced. Include details about what triggered your anger and how you responded. Over time, this journal can reveal patterns and trends in your emotional responses, providing valuable insights for anger management.

3. Mindful Breathing and Body Scan

Mindfulness practices, such as mindful breathing and body scans, aid in recognizing and managing emotional responses, including anger. Practice mindful breathing by:

- Finding a quiet and comfortable space to sit or lie down.

- Taking slow, deep breaths, focusing on each inhale and exhale.

- Paying attention to physical sensations, including tension and discomfort in the body.

During a body scan:

- Start at the top of your head and slowly move your focus down through your body, noting any areas of tension or discomfort.

- Pay attention to how different parts of your body feel and any sensations associated with anger or stress.

These exercises promote self-awareness and can be especially beneficial when practiced during or after moments of anger.

4. The ABCD Technique

The ABCD technique is a cognitive-behavioral exercise that helps individuals analyze their beliefs and thoughts related to anger. The acronym stands for:

- A: Activating Event (Identify the event or situation that triggered your anger)

- B: Beliefs (Examine your thoughts and beliefs about the event)

- C: Consequences (Note the emotional and behavioral consequences of your beliefs)

- D: Disputation (Challenge and reframe your irrational or unhelpful beliefs)

This exercise assists in uncovering and modifying thought patterns that contribute to anger and developing more balanced beliefs.

5. The Three-Step Process

This self-reflection exercise involves a three-step process aimed at understanding and managing anger:

- Pause: When you feel anger rising, take a moment to pause. Give yourself a chance to step back and assess the situation before reacting.

- Reflect: Use this pause to reflect on the situation. Identify the triggers and your immediate emotional and physical reactions to the event.

- Respond: After reflection, choose a response rather than reacting impulsively. Responding mindfully and constructively can reduce the intensity of your anger.

This exercise encourages a more measured and deliberate approach to handling anger-triggering situations.

In conclusion, journaling and self-reflection exercises are invaluable tools for understanding and managing anger. Journaling provides a platform for self-expression, exploration, and the identification of anger triggers and patterns. Self-reflection exercises complement journaling by offering structured techniques for delving deeper into emotional responses and exploring strategies for managing anger.

These practices enhance self-awareness, emotional intelligence, and the development of healthier coping mechanisms. Engaging in regular journaling and self-reflection exercises empowers individuals to navigate their emotions, including anger, with increased mindfulness, leading to improved emotional regulation and overall well-being.

In summary, the combined practices of journaling and self-reflection provide a foundation for individuals to explore their emotional landscape, understand their responses to anger, and develop effective strategies for managing and regulating their emotions.

CHAPTER FOUR

Cognitive Behavioral Techniques for Anger Control

Anger is a natural emotion, but when left unmanaged, it can become a disruptive and potentially harmful force in our lives. Cognitive-behavioral techniques (CBT) are powerful tools in the realm of anger management, offering structured methods to identify and modify thought patterns and behaviors associated with anger. This comprehensive exploration delves into the principles, methods, and efficacy of CBT in controlling and regulating anger.

Understanding Cognitive-Behavioral Techniques

Cognitive-behavioral techniques are grounded in the understanding that our thoughts, feelings, and behaviors are interconnected. The core principle of CBT is that our thoughts and beliefs influence our emotions and, in turn, affect our behaviors. By identifying and altering negative thought patterns and behaviors, CBT aims to bring about more balanced emotional responses, including managing anger.

The ABC Model

At the heart of CBT lies the ABC model, which stands for:

- A: Activating Event: The situation or trigger that initiates an emotional response.

- B: Beliefs: The thoughts and interpretations individuals hold about the activating event.

- C: Consequences: Emotional and behavioral outcomes that result from the beliefs held about the event.

This model illustrates that it is not the actual event (A) that directly causes an emotional reaction but the interpretation (B) of the event that leads to the emotional and behavioral consequences (C).

Identifying Irrational Beliefs

One of the core facets of CBT for anger control involves recognizing and challenging irrational beliefs that contribute to anger. These irrational beliefs often fall into categories known as "cognitive distortions," including:

1. All-or-Nothing Thinking: Seeing situations in extreme terms, black-or-white thinking without considering gray areas.

2. Overgeneralization: Making broad conclusions based on limited evidence or a single event.

3. Jumping to Conclusions: Assuming negative outcomes without evidence or facts.

4. Personalization: Taking responsibility for events beyond one's control or influence.

5. Magnification/Minimization: Exaggerating the importance of negative events or minimizing positive experiences.

6. Should Statements: Having rigid rules for oneself or others, leading to frustration and anger when these standards aren't met.

Cognitive Restructuring

Cognitive restructuring is a pivotal aspect of CBT for anger control. This process involves identifying, challenging, and altering irrational beliefs and thought patterns that contribute to anger. Techniques used in cognitive restructuring include:

1. Thought Monitoring: Individuals monitor and record their thoughts when they experience anger. They then analyze and challenge these thoughts to identify irrational or unhelpful patterns.

2. Evaluating Evidence: Encouraging individuals to examine the evidence supporting their beliefs. This technique helps in questioning the accuracy or validity of irrational beliefs and their basis in reality.

3. Alternative Explanations: Encouraging individuals to explore alternative, more balanced interpretations of events. This practice helps in developing a more realistic perspective and reducing the intensity of emotional responses.

4. Decatastrophizing: This technique involves challenging catastrophic thinking and reframing extreme predictions about negative outcomes. Individuals learn to view situations in a less threatening and more manageable light.

Behavioral Strategies

In addition to addressing cognitive patterns, CBT for anger control involves modifying behaviors that contribute to or result from anger. These behavioral strategies aim to promote healthier and more constructive responses to anger triggers. Techniques include:

1. Relaxation Techniques: Engaging in relaxation exercises such as deep breathing, progressive muscle relaxation, or mindfulness to reduce physiological arousal associated with anger.

2. Problem-Solving Skills: Developing effective problem-solving skills to address the root causes of anger triggers. This technique involves identifying problems, brainstorming solutions, and implementing those solutions.

3. Communication Skills: Enhancing communication and assertiveness skills to express emotions and needs in a non-confrontational and clear manner. Effective communication reduces the likelihood of misunderstandings that can lead to anger.

4. Behavioral Activation: Engaging in activities that promote positive emotions and well-being. Participation in enjoyable and rewarding activities can counteract the effects of anger-triggering situations.

Role-Playing and Behavioral Rehearsal

Role-playing and behavioral rehearsal are techniques often used in CBT to equip individuals with strategies for managing anger-inducing situations. By practicing and rehearsing responses in a safe environment, individuals can better manage their reactions when faced with real-life triggers.

1. Role-Playing Scenarios: Individuals and therapists act out scenarios that typically lead to anger. This allows individuals to practice responding differently, applying newly learned coping strategies.

2. Behavioral Rehearsal: In this technique, individuals repeatedly rehearse more adaptive responses to anger triggers. This practice involves visualizing the scenario and rehearsing appropriate responses until they become more automatic.

Anger Logs and Monitoring

Anger logs and monitoring are practical tools used in CBT to track and analyze anger triggers and responses. These techniques aid in recognizing patterns and developing strategies for better managing anger.

1. Anger Logs: Individuals maintain a log where they record details about anger-inducing situations, including triggers, thoughts, emotions, and responses. Anger logs help identify recurring patterns and trends.

2. Monitoring Emotional Responses: Individuals track their emotional responses to anger triggers using various rating scales. This monitoring provides insight into the intensity and duration of emotional reactions to specific triggers.

Social Skills Training

Social skills training is an integral part of CBT for anger control, focusing on enhancing interpersonal skills and communication to prevent or de-escalate anger-inducing situations.

1. Active Listening: Learning to listen and understand others' perspectives without interrupting or judging. Active listening helps in resolving conflicts and reducing misunderstandings.

2. Assertiveness Training: Teaching individuals to express their needs and feelings in a confident and assertive manner. Assertiveness helps individuals communicate effectively and reduce feelings of frustration that can lead to anger.

The Importance of Homework and Practice

Homework assignments and practice outside therapy sessions play a significant role in CBT for anger control. Therapists often assign tasks, exercises, and techniques for individuals to practice between sessions. Consistent practice reinforces learned skills and aids in the application of coping strategies in real-life situations.

The homework might involve journaling, role-playing, practicing relaxation techniques, or implementing strategies to manage anger triggers. Regular practice enhances the individual's ability to apply coping techniques and modify responses in everyday life.

Challenges and Considerations

Though CBT for anger control is highly effective, individuals might face certain challenges during the process:

1. Resistance to Change: Some individuals might find it challenging to modify entrenched beliefs and behaviors, leading to resistance during therapy.

2. Generalization of Skills: Applying learned skills and strategies in real-life situations outside of therapy can be challenging. The ability to generalize learned techniques to various scenarios is crucial for effective anger control.

3. Relapse and Persistence: Relapses in managing anger are common, and it's essential to persist in practicing learned skills and techniques to overcome setbacks.

4. Individual Differences: Different individuals respond differently to CBT techniques. Tailoring approaches to suit an individual's unique needs and learning styles is crucial for success.

Communication Skills: Assertiveness and Conflict Resolution

Effective communication is an essential component of interpersonal relationships, professional success, and personal well-being. Assertiveness, a vital communication skill, involves expressing one's thoughts, needs, and feelings in a direct, honest, and respectful manner. This comprehensive exploration delves into the principles, strategies, and importance of assertiveness in fostering healthy interactions and managing conflicts.

Assertiveness is a communication style that enables individuals to stand up for their rights and express their thoughts and feelings in a clear and respectful manner. It lies between two extremes: passive communication, where individuals avoid expressing their needs, and aggressive communication, which involves forceful and disrespectful behavior.

Core Principles of Assertiveness

1. Clear Communication: Assertive individuals express their thoughts and needs clearly, without ambiguity or uncertainty. They convey their message directly and effectively.

2. Respect for Others: While expressing their needs, assertive individuals respect the rights and opinions of others. They avoid being domineering or disregarding others' perspectives.

3. Honesty and Openness: Assertive communication involves being honest about one's thoughts and feelings without being hurtful or manipulative. Individuals express themselves openly while considering the feelings of others.

4. Conflict Resolution: Assertive communication facilitates conflict resolution by addressing issues directly and constructively. It promotes finding mutually beneficial solutions rather than dominating or giving in.

5. Personal Boundaries: Assertiveness involves setting and maintaining personal boundaries. It allows individuals to protect their rights without infringing on the rights of others.

The Importance of Assertiveness

Assertiveness is crucial in various aspects of life, offering numerous benefits:

1. Enhanced Self-Confidence: Assertive individuals have higher self-esteem and confidence as they can express themselves effectively.

2. Improved Relationships: Assertive communication fosters healthier relationships by promoting honesty, trust, and mutual respect.

3. Conflict Management: Assertiveness aids in resolving conflicts constructively, preventing issues from escalating and finding satisfactory resolutions.

4. Reduced Stress: Communicating assertively reduces stress by addressing issues directly and preventing internalized frustration.

Developing Assertiveness

1. Self-Awareness: Understanding one's needs, thoughts, and feelings is crucial for assertive communication. Self-awareness allows individuals to express themselves more effectively.

2. Practice Effective Communication: Individuals can practice stating their needs and thoughts clearly and respectfully. Role-playing various scenarios can help develop assertiveness skills.

3. Active Listening: Actively listening to others and respecting their viewpoints is essential in assertive communication. Acknowledging others' perspectives helps in mutual understanding.

4. Using "I" Statements: Using "I" statements instead of accusatory "you" statements can express feelings and thoughts without blaming others.

5. Seeking Support: Joining assertiveness training programs or seeking the guidance of a therapist can aid in developing and honing assertiveness skills.

Assertiveness at Work

In a professional setting, assertiveness is highly valuable. It allows individuals to express their ideas, provide feedback, and manage conflicts effectively. Assertive communication at work:

1. Promotes Effective Leadership: Assertive leaders can convey their vision and expectations clearly, fostering a productive work environment.

2. Facilitates Collaboration: Assertiveness encourages collaboration and teamwork by allowing individuals to express ideas and opinions freely.

3. Aids in Negotiation: In negotiations, assertive communication enables individuals to state their needs and reach mutually beneficial agreements.

4. Sets Boundaries: Assertive professionals can set boundaries, preventing exploitation or excessive work demands.

Challenges and Considerations in Developing Assertiveness

1. Overcoming Fear: Many individuals struggle with the fear of speaking up due to the fear of rejection or conflict. Overcoming this fear is crucial in developing assertiveness.

2. Balancing Assertiveness: Finding the balance between assertiveness and aggression can be challenging. Individuals should aim for directness while maintaining respect for others.

3. Cultural and Social Factors: Cultural and social norms may affect the degree of assertiveness deemed appropriate. Finding a balance within societal norms is essential.

Assertiveness is a valuable communication skill that fosters healthy relationships, effective conflict resolution, and personal well-being. By expressing needs and opinions directly and respectfully, individuals can enhance their self-confidence, improve relationships, and manage conflicts more constructively.

This comprehensive exploration delves into the principles, strategies, and importance of assertiveness in communication, offering individuals a guide to developing and applying this crucial skill in various aspects of life.

Anger-Reduction Methods and Coping Mechanisms

While experiencing anger isn't inherently problematic, unmanaged or excessive anger can lead to adverse consequences in personal relationships, work, and overall well-being. Anger-reduction methods and coping mechanisms play a vital role in managing and mitigating the impact of anger on individuals' lives.

When anger is left unaddressed or unmanaged, it can have wide-ranging effects on individuals, both emotionally and physically. Uncontrolled anger can contribute to increased stress, elevated blood pressure, and heightened risk of heart disease. It can also strain personal relationships, leading to conflicts and social isolation. Additionally, prolonged anger may contribute to mental health issues such as anxiety and depression.

Anger-Reduction Methods

1. Mindfulness Practices: Mindfulness involves being present in the moment without judgment. Mindfulness practices, such as meditation and deep breathing exercises, help individuals manage their emotional responses by promoting self-awareness and emotional regulation. By focusing on the present moment, individuals can recognize and mitigate their anger triggers.

2. Relaxation Techniques: Engaging in relaxation exercises, such as progressive muscle relaxation, visualization, or yoga, can help reduce physiological arousal associated with anger. These techniques promote a sense of calm and reduce the body's stress response, aiding in managing anger.

3. Cognitive Restructuring: Cognitive techniques focus on identifying and challenging irrational thoughts or beliefs that contribute to anger. By reframing negative thoughts and practicing positive thinking, individuals can manage their emotional responses more effectively.

4. Physical Exercise: Regular physical activity is a beneficial way to reduce stress and release pent-up tension associated with anger. Exercise helps regulate emotions and promotes overall well-being.

5. Healthy Expression of Anger: Learning to express anger in a healthy and constructive manner is crucial. Verbalizing feelings assertively but not aggressively, while actively listening to others, can prevent conflicts and reduce the intensity of anger.

6. Journaling: Writing about anger triggers, emotional responses, and personal reflections is a helpful way to understand patterns and gain insights into one's anger. Journaling provides an outlet for emotional expression and aids in identifying triggers.

Coping Mechanisms for Anger Management

1. Time-Outs: Taking a break or time-out when feeling angry can help individuals calm down before responding impulsively. Stepping away from a heated situation allows for reflection and prevents hasty reactions.

2. Deep Breathing Exercises: Deep breathing exercises, such as diaphragmatic breathing, aid in reducing the physiological response to anger. Focusing on slow, deep breaths can help restore a sense of calm and reduce tension.

3. Positive Self-Talk: Utilizing positive self-talk involves using affirmations or positive statements to counteract negative thoughts associated with anger. Affirming statements can help reframe the perspective and reduce the intensity of anger.

4. Seeking Support and Counseling: Seeking professional help from therapists or support groups can provide guidance and tools for managing anger. Therapy allows individuals to explore the root causes of their anger and develop effective coping strategies.

5. Healthy Lifestyle Changes: Making lifestyle changes, such as getting adequate sleep, maintaining a balanced diet, and reducing stress, supports overall emotional well-being and contributes to better anger management.

6. Assertiveness and Communication Skills: Developing assertiveness and effective communication skills aids in expressing needs and opinions without aggressive behavior, thus reducing potential conflicts and anger triggers.

7. Setting Boundaries: Establishing clear boundaries and limitations in personal and professional relationships helps prevent situations that may lead to anger or resentment.

8. Humor and Distraction: Engaging in activities that bring joy or humor, such as watching a comedy or participating in a hobby, can serve as a distraction and alleviate anger by shifting focus.

Integrating Coping Mechanisms into Daily Life

Successfully integrating these anger-reduction methods and coping mechanisms into daily life involves consistent practice and perseverance. Developing a routine that incorporates these strategies in various life situations is key. Additionally, it's essential to recognize that different coping mechanisms work differently for each individual. Experimentation and finding what works best for personal needs and preferences is crucial.

Challenges in Implementing Coping Mechanisms

There are several challenges individuals may face in implementing coping mechanisms for anger reduction:

1. Consistency and Commitment: Developing new habits and coping strategies requires consistency and commitment. It can be challenging to maintain these practices consistently.

2. Recognizing Triggers: Identifying and understanding personal anger triggers can be difficult. It takes time and self-reflection to recognize and address these triggers effectively.

3. Social and Environmental Factors: Social situations or environmental stressors can pose challenges in practicing coping mechanisms. Finding ways to manage anger in various settings can be challenging.

4. Personal Resistance to Change: Resistance to change or fear of adopting new coping mechanisms may hinder progress. Accepting and adapting to new practices may take time and effort.

Anger is a complex emotion that, when unmanaged, can have detrimental effects on personal well-being and relationships. Utilizing anger-reduction methods and coping mechanisms is crucial in managing and mitigating the impact of anger. Through mindfulness practices, relaxation

techniques, cognitive restructuring, and healthy expression of anger, individuals can effectively manage their emotional responses. Implementing coping mechanisms such as time-outs, deep breathing exercises, positive self-talk, and seeking support allows for healthier emotional regulation.

This comprehensive exploration has outlined various anger-reduction methods and coping mechanisms, emphasizing the importance of incorporating these strategies into daily life for enhanced emotional regulation and overall well-being.

CHAPTER FIVE

Impact of Anger on Relationships: Romantic, Family, and Friendships

Unmanaged or excessive anger can have significant implications on relationships, be it romantic, familial, or friendships. This extensive exploration delves into the multifaceted impact of anger on these relationships, its underlying causes, and strategies for managing anger to maintain healthier connections.

Anger in relationships is a complex emotion that, when left unaddressed or unmanaged, can breed resentment, conflict, and deterioration of the relationship. Understanding the impact of anger on different types of relationships is essential for fostering healthy and harmonious connections.

Romantic Relationships

In romantic relationships, anger has a profound impact on the dynamics and emotional landscape:

1. Conflict Resolution: While occasional disagreements are common in relationships, unresolved anger and frequent conflict can lead to emotional distance and erosion of trust between partners.

2. Communication Breakdown: Unmanaged anger often results in breakdowns in communication. Hostility, passive-aggressiveness, or intense arguments hinder effective dialogue, making it challenging to resolve issues amicably.

3. Intimacy and Trust: Continual anger may erode intimacy and trust in romantic relationships. Unaddressed anger leads to emotional distance, making it challenging to foster an environment of vulnerability and closeness.

4. Cycle of Resentment: Recurring episodes of unresolved anger and fights lead to a cycle of resentment. Lingering anger can accumulate and negatively impact the relationship's emotional climate.

Family Relationships

Anger within familial bonds impacts the family dynamic in several ways:

1. Parent-Child Relationships: Unmanaged anger from parents can adversely affect children's emotional well-being. It can instill fear, erode self-esteem, and hinder healthy parent-child communication.

2. Sibling Relationships: Anger between siblings may lead to prolonged conflicts, strained communication, and disrupted familial harmony. It can create lasting tensions and animosity.

3. Extended Family Relationships: Anger may impact relationships within extended families, causing rifts or strained interactions during family gatherings or events.

4. Generational Impact: Patterns of anger within families can carry forward across generations, affecting how individuals perceive and handle anger in their own relationships and interactions.

Friendships

Anger within friendships poses its own set of challenges:

1. Strained Dynamics: Unmanaged anger may lead to fractured friendships. Continuous conflicts, disagreements, or unresolved issues can strain the relationship, potentially leading to its dissolution.

2. Communication Barriers: Anger can create communication barriers in friendships, making it difficult to express concerns, leading to misunderstandings and misinterpretations.

3. Trust and Reliability: Excessive anger or frequent conflicts may impact trust and reliability in friendships. It can strain the foundation of trust and mutual support.

4. Emotional Well-being: Negative emotions stemming from anger can take a toll on individual well-being within friendships, potentially impacting the mental and emotional health of both friends.

Causes of Anger in Relationships

Understanding the underlying causes of anger in relationships is crucial to address and manage this emotion effectively:

1. Communication Breakdown: Poor communication, misinterpretations, or misunderstanding can lead to unresolved issues and pent-up frustration, fueling anger.

2. Unmet Expectations: When individuals have unmet or unrealistic expectations from their relationships, it can lead to disappointment and subsequent anger.

3. Conflict of Values: Differences in beliefs, values, or priorities can create friction, leading to anger and conflicts in relationships.

4. Stress and External Factors: Stress from external sources, such as work, financial strain, or health issues, can lead to heightened emotional responses, including anger, within relationships.

Impact of Unmanaged Anger

1. Deterioration of Trust: Continuous unresolved anger erodes trust within relationships, making it challenging to rely on one another and fostering a sense of insecurity.

2. Emotional Distance: Unaddressed anger leads to emotional distance, preventing genuine emotional connection and closeness within relationships.

3. Resentment and Bitterness: Lingering anger and unresolved conflicts lead to feelings of resentment and bitterness, affecting the emotional climate of the relationship.

4. Impact on Mental Health: Prolonged exposure to anger within relationships can have adverse effects on mental health, leading to stress, anxiety, and even depression.

Strategies for Managing Anger in Relationships

1. Effective Communication: Open and honest communication allows for the expression of feelings and concerns, minimizing misunderstandings and resentment.

2. Conflict Resolution Skills: Developing effective conflict resolution skills helps in addressing issues constructively, preventing prolonged conflicts.

3. Anger Management Techniques: Individuals can engage in anger management programs or therapy to learn constructive ways to manage and express their anger in relationships.

4. Empathy and Understanding: Cultivating empathy and understanding for the other person's feelings aids in managing conflicts and finding amicable solutions.

5. Setting Boundaries: Establishing and respecting personal boundaries in relationships is crucial for managing conflicts and avoiding situations that may lead to anger.

6. Seeking Professional Help: In cases of persistent or severe anger issues, seeking the guidance of a therapist or counselor can provide effective tools for managing anger within relationships.

Anger, when unmanaged, significantly impacts various relationships, be it romantic, familial, or friendships. Understanding the causes and implications of anger in relationships is crucial for fostering healthy and harmonious connections. Implementing effective communication, conflict resolution skills, and anger management techniques aids in managing and mitigating the impact of anger on relationships, fostering healthier and more fulfilling connections.

Healthy Conflict Resolution in Personal Connections

Conflict is an inevitable part of human relationships. Whether in romantic partnerships, family dynamics, friendships, or any social interactions, conflicts are a natural occurrence arising from differences in opinions, needs, and expectations. How individuals manage these conflicts determines the health and longevity of their relationships. Healthy conflict resolution is a crucial skill that enables individuals to address disagreements constructively, fostering understanding, growth, and stronger connections.

Conflict in personal connections arises from various sources. It might stem from differences in beliefs, values, expectations, or various other individual characteristics. It's not merely a clash of opposing ideas but also the clash of emotions, perceptions, and priorities within the relationships. Conflict isn't inherently detrimental; it's the way it's handled that determines its impact.

Healthy conflict resolution is pivotal in maintaining and nurturing relationships. It allows individuals to navigate disagreements while preserving mutual respect and understanding. Successfully resolving conflicts fosters stronger connections and trust among individuals. It's a crucial skill that not only resolves issues but also strengthens relationships by promoting open communication and understanding.

Characteristics of Healthy Conflict Resolution

1. Effective Communication: Open and honest communication is the foundation of resolving conflicts in a healthy manner. It allows individuals to express their thoughts and feelings without judgment.

2. Respectful Dialogue: Engaging in respectful and considerate communication ensures that conflicting parties address issues without belittling or disrespecting each other.

3. Active Listening: The art of active listening, where individuals genuinely hear and comprehend the other person's viewpoint, is vital. It promotes understanding and empathizing with their feelings and concerns.

4. Empathy and Understanding: The ability to put oneself in the other person's shoes fosters empathy, leading to a deeper understanding of their perspective.

5. Collaborative Problem-Solving: Rather than trying to win, a collaborative approach to solving problems ensures that both parties work together towards a resolution, focusing on mutual benefit.

Strategies for Healthy Conflict Resolution

1. Identify the Issue: Pinpoint the exact issue causing the conflict. Sometimes, conflicts might stem from underlying causes that need addressing for a satisfactory resolution.

2. Express Feelings and Needs: Being able to communicate one's feelings and needs openly and honestly is crucial for resolution.

3. Active Listening and Understanding: Actively listening and understanding the other party's perspective fosters an environment for healthy conflict resolution.

4. Avoid Blame and Criticism: Instead of blaming each other, focus on the issue at hand. Avoid criticism or personal attacks that can intensify the conflict.

5. Brainstorm Solutions: Collaboratively generating potential solutions helps in finding an agreeable resolution to the conflict.

6. Evaluate and Choose Solutions: After brainstorming, evaluating and selecting the most viable solution mutually beneficial to both parties ensures a meaningful resolution.

Conflict Resolution in Romantic Relationships

Conflict resolution in romantic relationships holds great significance. When conflicts arise in a romantic partnership, the stakes are high due to the emotional investment involved. Healthy conflict resolution in romantic relationships involves effective communication, empathy, and mutual respect. Couples need to learn to navigate disagreements while maintaining the integrity of the relationship.

Open and honest communication in a romantic relationship ensures that both partners feel heard and understood. It fosters an environment of trust, allowing for deeper emotional connections.

The ability to understand each other's perspective and empathize with their feelings is crucial. It helps in de-escalating conflicts and finding resolutions that satisfy both partners.

Conflict resolution in romantic relationships also involves the art of compromise. Being able to meet in the middle and find solutions that serve both partners is a skill that strengthens the relationship.

Conflict resolution isn't about eliminating disagreements; it's about navigating them in a healthy manner that promotes understanding and strengthens the bond between partners.

Conflict Resolution in Family Dynamics

In family dynamics, conflicts can arise due to differences in opinions, values, and generational gaps. Healthy conflict resolution within families is crucial for maintaining strong bonds and fostering a harmonious environment.

Open communication within families ensures that each member feels valued and heard. It prevents conflicts from escalating and helps in finding resolutions that satisfy everyone.

Respect for individual differences is essential within family conflicts. Acknowledging and respecting each member's unique beliefs and values helps prevent tensions and fosters a more harmonious environment.

Forgiveness and understanding within families allow conflicts to be resolved more amicably. Families that practice forgiveness and understanding exhibit stronger bonds and healthier relationships.

Conflict resolution in families involves setting and respecting personal boundaries. It prevents conflicts that may arise from overstepping individual limits and ensures a more peaceful coexistence.

Conflict Resolution in Friendships

Friendships might encounter conflicts due to misunderstandings, miscommunications, or differing opinions. Navigating conflicts in friendships is crucial for maintaining trust and nurturing the relationship.

Healthy conflict resolution in friendships involves honest and respectful communication. Friends need to express their feelings and needs without belittling each other.

Empathy and understanding within friendships are vital. It fosters a deeper understanding of each other's perspectives, allowing conflicts to be addressed constructively.

Addressing conflicts promptly within friendships prevents them from festering and causing long-term damage. It fosters an environment of trust and openness between friends.

Forgiveness and mutual support within friendships ensure that conflicts are resolved more effectively, allowing the friendship to continue thriving.

The Role of Compromise in Conflict Resolution

Compromise is a fundamental aspect of healthy conflict resolution. It requires individuals to set aside their personal interests for the greater good of the relationship or the issue at hand.

Finding a middle ground where both parties feel heard and considered is the essence of compromise. It fosters understanding and prevents a win-lose situation.

Shared decision-making in conflicts ensures that both parties have an equal say in the resolution, maintaining a balanced power dynamic.

Compromise encourages cooperation and collaboration, leading to resolutions that are mutually satisfying and beneficial to both parties.

Barriers to Effective Conflict Resolution

Various barriers hinder healthy conflict resolution:

1. Communication Issues: Ineffective communication or unwillingness to communicate openly is a significant barrier to resolving conflicts.

2. Ego and Stubbornness: Stubbornness and an unwillingness to consider other perspectives can hinder healthy conflict resolution.

3. Unresolved Issues: Previous unresolved conflicts or underlying tensions can become barriers in addressing new conflicts.

4. Emotional Regulation: Inability to manage emotions or reactive behavior during conflicts can impede effective resolution.

Conflict is an inevitable aspect of human relationships, but how individuals manage and resolve conflicts determines the health and strength of their connections. Healthy conflict resolution involves effective communication, empathy, and the willingness to compromise. Whether it's in romantic relationships, family dynamics, friendships, or any social interactions, mastering the art of healthy conflict resolution is key to fostering understanding, growth, and stronger relationships.

Rebuilding Trust and Repairing Relationships

Trust serves as the cornerstone of healthy relationships. It's the foundation upon which intimacy, understanding, and emotional connection are built. When trust is compromised or broken, relationships face turmoil, leading to strain, emotional distance, and fractured connections. Rebuilding trust is a critical endeavor in restoring relationships to a healthier state.

Trust is multifaceted and complex. It encompasses emotional, behavioral, and cognitive components. Emotional trust involves the feelings of security and safety in a relationship, while behavioral trust is reliant on consistent actions and reliability. Cognitive trust involves belief in the other person's integrity and honesty.

The Impact of Broken Trust in Relationships

When trust is compromised, relationships face various challenges:

1. Emotional Distance: Breaches in trust often lead to emotional distance between individuals. The wounded party might feel unsafe or guarded, preventing emotional vulnerability.

2. Loss of Intimacy: Broken trust can erode the level of intimacy and connection within relationships, hindering the closeness between individuals.

3. Resentment and Hurt: Individuals who have faced broken trust often harbor feelings of resentment, hurt, and disappointment, affecting the emotional climate of the relationship.

4. Communication Breakdown: Trust issues often lead to communication breakdown, inhibiting open and honest dialogue.

The Process of Rebuilding Trust

1. Acknowledgment and Acceptance: Acknowledging the breach in trust and accepting responsibility for the hurt caused is the initial step in rebuilding trust. It's essential for the offending party to acknowledge the impact of their actions.

2. Open Communication: Open and honest communication is crucial in addressing trust issues. Both parties need to express their feelings, concerns, and needs openly and respectfully.

3. Apology and Forgiveness: Offering a sincere apology and seeking forgiveness is vital. The offended party, in turn, needs to be willing to forgive, setting the foundation for healing.

4. Consistent Actions: Consistency in actions is key in rebuilding trust. The offending party needs to demonstrate reliability and commitment to change.

5. Empathy and Understanding: Developing empathy and understanding for the hurt and pain caused is crucial for healing and rebuilding trust.

6. Time and Patience: Rebuilding trust is a gradual process that requires time and patience. Rushing the process might hinder its effectiveness.

Factors Affecting the Process of Rebuilding Trust

1. Severity of the Breach: The gravity of the breach in trust determines the complexity and duration of the rebuilding process.

2. Individual Differences: Each person responds differently to breaches in trust. Their past experiences and personalities play a significant role in the rebuilding process.

3. Level of Commitment: The commitment of both parties to rebuild trust significantly impacts the process. It requires dedication and effort from all parties involved.

4. External Support and Guidance: Seeking external support from therapists, counselors, or support groups can aid in the rebuilding process.

Rebuilding Trust in Romantic Relationships

Rebuilding trust in romantic relationships involves:

1. Open and Honest Dialogue: Communicating openly about feelings, concerns, and needs is crucial in the healing process.

2. Apology and Forgiveness: Offering a sincere apology and being open to forgiveness is pivotal for healing in romantic relationships.

3. Commitment to Change: Demonstrating consistent actions and commitment to change is vital in rebuilding trust in romantic relationships.

4. Re-establishing Emotional Connection: Efforts to re-establish emotional connection and intimacy can aid in the rebuilding process.

Rebuilding Trust in Familial Relationships

Healing trust issues within family dynamics includes:

1. Acknowledgment of Hurt: Acknowledging the hurt caused and understanding the impact of actions is the foundation for rebuilding trust.

2. Open Communication: Engaging in open and respectful dialogue helps in addressing issues constructively within families.

3. Developing Empathy and Understanding: Cultivating empathy and understanding for each other's feelings and concerns is vital in rebuilding trust within families.

4. Time and Patience: Rebuilding trust within families is a gradual process that requires patience and perseverance.

Rebuilding Trust in Friendships

Rebuilding trust within friendships involves:

1. Open Communication and Apology: Honest communication and offering a sincere apology is crucial in restoring trust within friendships.

2. Consistent Actions and Reliability: Demonstrating consistent actions and reliability is key in rebuilding trust among friends.

3. Forgiveness and Understanding: Being open to forgiveness and understanding helps in the healing process within friendships.

4. Re-establishing Emotional Connection: Efforts to re-establish an emotional connection and support are vital for rebuilding trust among friends.

Challenges in Rebuilding Trust and Repairing Relationships

1. Residual Hurt and Resentment: The lingering feelings of hurt and resentment might hinder the process of rebuilding trust.

2. Patience and Time: Rebuilding trust is a gradual process that requires time and patience, often testing the commitment of all parties involved.

3. Communication Barriers: Communication breakdown or misunderstandings might impede the rebuilding process, making it essential to address such barriers.

4. External Influences: External factors, such as opinions of others or societal norms, might affect the rebuilding process, requiring a focus on the core relationship.

Rebuilding trust and repairing relationships is a multifaceted journey requiring commitment, empathy, and consistent effort. The process of rebuilding trust involves acknowledgment, open communication, consistent actions, and a genuine commitment to healing. Whether in romantic relationships, family dynamics, friendships, or any social context, the significance of trust in fostering healthy, resilient connections cannot be overstated. Rebuilding trust is a process that requires time, patience, and dedication from all involved parties to restore the emotional connection and strengthen relationships.

CHAPTER SIX

Stress-Reduction Techniques and Lifestyle Adjustments

In today's fast-paced world, stress has become a prevalent aspect of daily life for many. While some stress is inevitable and even beneficial in small doses, chronic stress can have detrimental effects on mental, emotional, and physical health. This extensive exploration delves into stress-reduction techniques and lifestyle adjustments, focusing on proactive measures individuals can adopt to manage stress and lead a more balanced and fulfilling life.

Stress is the body's natural response to perceived threats or demands, triggering a cascade of physiological and psychological reactions. When stress becomes chronic, it can lead to a range of health issues, including anxiety, depression, cardiovascular problems, and weakened immunity.

Understanding the sources of stress in one's life is the first step toward managing it. Stressors can be varied and include work-related pressures, financial concerns, relationship issues, health problems, or lifestyle factors.

Stress-Reduction Techniques

1. Mindfulness and Meditation: Practicing mindfulness and meditation allows individuals to focus on the present moment, reducing anxiety and promoting relaxation. Mindfulness-based stress reduction techniques have shown to be effective in managing stress.

2. Deep Breathing and Relaxation Exercises: Deep breathing exercises help activate the body's relaxation response, lowering stress levels. Techniques like progressive muscle relaxation or guided imagery aid in promoting relaxation and reducing tension.

3. Physical Exercise: Regular physical activity is a potent stress reducer. Exercise releases endorphins, improving mood, reducing anxiety, and enhancing overall well-being.

4. Yoga and Tai Chi: These mind-body practices combine physical postures, breathing exercises, and meditation, providing a holistic approach to stress reduction and relaxation.

5. Art and Music Therapy: Engaging in creative activities like painting, drawing, or playing musical instruments can be therapeutic, offering a constructive outlet for stress relief.

Lifestyle Adjustments for Stress Management

1. Healthy Diet: A balanced and nutritious diet plays a crucial role in stress management. Foods rich in omega-3 fatty acids, complex carbohydrates, and antioxidants can positively impact mood and stress levels.

2. Adequate Sleep: Quality sleep is vital for stress management. Establishing a regular sleep routine and ensuring a restful environment can significantly reduce stress levels.

3. Time Management: Effective time management can reduce stress. Prioritizing tasks, setting realistic goals, and learning to say no when necessary can help in managing stress more effectively.

4. Social Support: Building a strong support network helps in managing stress. Connecting with friends, family, or support groups can provide emotional support and aid in stress reduction.

5. Setting Boundaries: Establishing personal boundaries, both at work and in personal life, prevents overload and promotes a healthier balance.

6. Mindful Technology Use: Limiting screen time and engaging in digital detoxes can significantly reduce stress, allowing for more time to relax and focus on other activities.

Professional Support and Therapies

1. Counseling and Therapy: Seeking professional help from counselors or therapists aids in managing stress and offers strategies to cope with life's challenges.

2. Stress-Management Programs: Participating in stress-management programs provides valuable tools and techniques to effectively manage stress.

3. Biofeedback and Relaxation Techniques: Learning biofeedback techniques can assist in managing stress by controlling bodily functions and reducing tension.

Nature and Stress Reduction

Spending time in nature, also known as ecotherapy, is an effective stress-reduction strategy. Being in natural surroundings, whether hiking in forests, spending time near water bodies, or gardening, has shown to have a calming effect on the mind and body.

Workplace Stress Management

Employers are increasingly recognizing the importance of addressing stress in the workplace. Introducing stress-reduction programs, promoting flexible work hours, providing mental health support, and encouraging a positive work culture can significantly reduce stress among employees.

Cognitive Behavioral Techniques

Cognitive behavioral techniques teach individuals to identify and challenge negative thought patterns, aiding in stress reduction. By changing thoughts and behaviors, individuals can manage stress more effectively.

Mindfulness-Based Stress Reduction (MBSR) Programs

MBSR programs focus on mindfulness meditation and yoga. They have proven effective in reducing stress, anxiety, and improving overall mental well-being.

In our fast-paced society, stress has become a common companion. However, proactive measures, such as mindfulness practices, lifestyle adjustments, professional support, and nature engagement, can significantly alleviate stress. It's crucial to identify stressors, adopt stress-reduction techniques, and make lifestyle adjustments to lead a more balanced, healthier, and fulfilling life.

This extensive exploration has highlighted a wide array of stress-reduction techniques and lifestyle adjustments, emphasizing the importance of proactive stress management in fostering overall well-being and leading a more fulfilling life.

Emotional Regulation Exercises and Coping Strategies

Emotions play a central role in our daily experiences, influencing our thoughts, behaviors, and interactions. Emotional regulation refers to the ability to effectively manage and control one's emotions. This comprehensive exploration delves into emotional regulation exercises and coping strategies, providing a range of techniques to understand, manage, and respond to emotions in a healthy and constructive manner.

Emotional regulation encompasses the ability to recognize, understand, and manage emotions. It involves the process of adjusting the intensity, duration, and expression of emotions. Developing effective emotional regulation skills aids in navigating various life situations with more resilience and adaptability.

Emotional regulation significantly influences mental health, interpersonal relationships, and overall well-being. Individuals with effective emotional regulation skills often experience reduced stress, improved relationships, and enhanced mental and emotional health.

Emotional Regulation Exercises

1. Mindfulness Practices: Engaging in mindfulness exercises allows individuals to become more aware of their emotions and thoughts. Techniques such as mindful breathing, body scan, and focused attention on the present moment aid in regulating emotions.

2. Emotion Labeling and Recognition: Developing the ability to identify and label specific emotions helps individuals manage and process their feelings more effectively. This might involve creating an emotion journal to record and recognize emotions.

3. Deep Breathing and Relaxation Techniques: Deep breathing exercises activate the body's relaxation response, assisting in calming emotions and reducing stress. Progressive muscle relaxation and guided imagery are effective relaxation techniques.

4. Cognitive Restructuring: This technique involves challenging and reframing negative thought patterns. By changing thought processes, individuals can alter emotional responses to various situations.

5. Sensory Grounding Techniques: Sensory grounding involves focusing on the immediate environment through the senses to alleviate overwhelming emotions. Techniques might include focusing on textures, colors, scents, or sounds in the present moment.

6. Physical Activity and Exercise: Regular physical exercise is a potent tool for emotional regulation. It helps in releasing endorphins, improving mood, and reducing stress.

Coping Strategies for Emotional Regulation

1. Journaling and Writing: Expressive writing allows individuals to articulate their thoughts and emotions, providing a healthy outlet for processing and regulating emotions.

2. Social Support and Communication: Seeking support from friends, family, or support groups helps individuals manage emotions. Open and honest communication aids in processing feelings and finding solutions.

3. Expressive Arts and Creative Outlets: Engaging in creative activities, such as painting, drawing, music, or dancing, serves as a constructive outlet for managing and expressing emotions.

4. Mindfulness and Meditation: Regular practice of mindfulness and meditation fosters emotional regulation by developing present-moment awareness and reducing emotional reactivity.

5. Self-Compassion and Acceptance: Cultivating self-compassion and acceptance aids in emotional regulation. Understanding that it's natural to experience various emotions helps individuals manage them more effectively.

6. Problem-Solving Strategies: Developing problem-solving skills helps individuals manage the stress and emotional impact of challenges by breaking down problems into manageable parts and finding solutions.

The Role of Therapy and Professional Support

Therapy, such as cognitive-behavioral therapy (CBT) or dialectical behavior therapy (DBT), offers effective tools and strategies for managing and regulating emotions. These therapies provide structured approaches to help individuals navigate their emotional landscape more effectively.

Adverse Effects of Poor Emotional Regulation

Poor emotional regulation can lead to various adverse effects, including increased stress, anxiety, relationship conflicts, impulsive behavior, and mental health issues such as depression or mood disorders.

Emotional Regulation in Different Settings

1. Workplace and Stress Management: Effective emotional regulation at the workplace is vital for stress management. It involves dealing with pressures, handling conflicts, and maintaining a healthy work-life balance.

2. Family Dynamics and Interpersonal Relationships: Emotional regulation in family dynamics aids in managing conflicts, fostering understanding, and maintaining healthier relationships.

3. Friendships and Social Interactions: Emotionally regulating oneself in friendships helps in maintaining open communication, resolving conflicts, and fostering strong bonds.

Challenges in Emotional Regulation

Challenges in emotional regulation might include the difficulty in identifying or expressing emotions, past trauma impacting emotional responses, or environmental stressors affecting emotional regulation.

Cultural and Individual Differences

Cultural differences and individual backgrounds might influence the way people perceive, express, or manage emotions. Understanding these differences is crucial in developing effective emotional regulation techniques.

The Role of Self-Care in Emotional Regulation

Self-care practices, such as maintaining a healthy lifestyle, engaging in hobbies, setting boundaries, and seeking social support, are vital in regulating emotions and promoting mental health.

Effective emotional regulation is essential for mental and emotional well-being, influencing relationships and overall quality of life. Employing a range of techniques, from mindfulness and relaxation exercises to coping strategies and professional support, individuals can learn to manage and regulate their emotions more effectively.

Building Resilience in Handling Life's Challenges

Resilience, in its essence, is the capacity to adapt, grow, and thrive in the face of adversity, trauma, stress, or significant life challenges. It's not merely the ability to bounce back but to progress beyond previous levels of functioning, becoming stronger and more adaptable as a result of the adversity encountered. This extensive exploration delves into the significance of building resilience and offers strategies for developing this crucial trait in effectively navigating life's challenges.

Resilience is a dynamic quality that individuals can develop over time. It involves mental fortitude, emotional strength, and adaptive strategies to face and overcome adversities. Resilient individuals possess the ability to maintain a positive outlook, cope with stress, and adapt to difficult circumstances.

The Importance of Resilience in Handling Life's Challenges

Resilience plays a pivotal role in how individuals approach, confront, and overcome life's challenges. It enables individuals to bounce back from setbacks, develop problem-solving skills, and maintain emotional stability in difficult situations.

Key Components of Resilience

1. Emotional Regulation: The ability to manage and regulate emotions effectively is a crucial component of resilience. Emotionally resilient individuals can navigate strong emotions without being overwhelmed by them.

2. Positive Mindset and Adaptability: Having a positive outlook and the ability to adapt to changing situations are key aspects of resilience. Individuals with a growth mindset view challenges as opportunities for growth and learning.

3. Coping Strategies and Problem-Solving Skills: Resilient individuals possess effective coping mechanisms and problem-solving skills that help them navigate and overcome challenges.

4. Social Support and Connections: Building and maintaining a strong support network is an essential component of resilience. Having people to turn to in times of adversity aids in managing challenges effectively.

Factors Contributing to Resilience

1. Supportive Relationships: Having strong and supportive relationships fosters resilience. Support from family, friends, or a community is crucial in facing and overcoming life's challenges.

2. Emotional Intelligence: High emotional intelligence aids in understanding and managing emotions, developing empathy, and effective communication, contributing to resilience.

3. Problem-Solving Skills: Developing problem-solving abilities helps in managing challenges more effectively and contributes to building resilience.

4. Optimism and Positive Mindset: A positive outlook and an optimistic approach to life's challenges enhance resilience, allowing individuals to maintain hope and motivation in difficult times.

5. Coping Mechanisms: Developing healthy coping mechanisms, such as mindfulness, relaxation techniques, and self-care practices, contributes to building resilience.

Strategies for Building Resilience

1. Cultivating Positive Relationships: Building and maintaining positive relationships creates a support system that aids in resilience.

2. Developing Problem-Solving Skills: Enhancing problem-solving skills helps in navigating challenges and adversity more effectively.

3. Adopting a Growth Mindset: Cultivating a growth mindset allows individuals to see challenges as opportunities for learning and growth.

4. Self-Reflection and Self-Awareness: Developing self-awareness aids in understanding one's reactions and emotions, contributing to effective coping strategies.

5. Mindfulness and Stress-Reduction Techniques: Practicing mindfulness and stress reduction techniques fosters emotional regulation and resilience.

Resilience in Specific Contexts

1. Resilience in Work and Career: Building resilience in the workplace aids in managing stress, adapting to change, and overcoming obstacles.

2. Resilience in Relationships: Developing resilience in relationships helps individuals navigate conflicts, setbacks, and maintain healthy connections.

3. Resilience in Health Challenges: Resilience aids in facing health challenges by providing the mental and emotional strength necessary to cope and adapt to the situation.

4. Resilience in Personal Development: Building resilience aids in personal growth, as it allows individuals to face challenges, learn from experiences, and progress.

Barriers to Building Resilience

Barriers to building resilience can significantly impact an individual's ability to adapt, thrive, and recover from adversities. These barriers hinder the development and strengthening of resilience, making it more challenging for individuals to bounce back from life's difficulties. Understanding these obstacles is essential in addressing and overcoming them. Some common barriers to building resilience include:

1. Lack of Supportive Relationships: A lack of positive and supportive connections with family, friends, or community can impede resilience-building, as strong relationships play a fundamental role in navigating challenges.

2. Trauma and Adverse Experiences: Past traumas, such as abuse, neglect, or significant adverse experiences, can hinder the development of resilience, impacting emotional regulation and coping mechanisms.

3. Limited Coping Skills: Insufficient skills to manage stress, solve problems, or regulate emotions can pose a significant barrier to building resilience.

4. Negative Thought Patterns: Persistent negative thinking or a fixed mindset can hinder the development of resilience, affecting an individual's ability to view challenges as opportunities for growth.

5. Environmental Stressors: Challenging living conditions, economic hardships, or chronic stress in the environment can impede resilience-building efforts.

6. Lack of Access to Resources: Limited access to mental health resources, educational opportunities, or support services can hinder resilience development.

Recognizing and addressing these barriers is crucial in fostering resilience. Overcoming these challenges involves creating supportive environments, teaching coping strategies, promoting positive thinking, and offering access to resources to aid individuals in developing and strengthening their resilience.

The Role of Failure in Building Resilience

The role of failure in building resilience is fundamental to personal growth and adaptability. Failure, often perceived negatively, serves as a pivotal teacher in life, offering valuable lessons and opportunities for learning and improvement. When faced with setbacks or failures, individuals encounter a chance to develop resilience, problem-solving skills, and emotional fortitude.

Experiencing failure introduces individuals to adversity, enabling them to build resilience by learning how to cope, adapt, and persevere in the face of challenges. It fosters the ability to bounce back, acquire new insights, and develop a positive mindset toward setbacks.

The process of confronting and overcoming failure cultivates resilience by teaching individuals to embrace mistakes as stepping stones toward success. It encourages a growth mindset, where failure is not viewed as an endpoint but as a crucial part of the learning process. This outlook helps individuals become more adaptable, persistent, and open to new opportunities for growth and self-improvement.

In essence, failure acts as a catalyst for resilience-building, shaping individuals to face challenges with determination and a willingness to learn from setbacks, ultimately strengthening their ability to navigate life's obstacles and thrive in the face of adversity.

The Link Between Resilience and Mental Health

Resilience is closely linked to mental health. Individuals with higher levels of resilience are better equipped to manage stress, anxiety, and depression, as they possess adaptive coping mechanisms.

The link between resilience and mental health is a crucial connection that significantly influences an individual's ability to cope with stress, adversity, and overall well-being. Resilience acts as a protective factor, impacting mental health positively and contributing to emotional strength, adaptability, and coping strategies.

A resilient mindset can mitigate the impact of stress, trauma, or adverse life events on mental health. It aids in managing and regulating emotions, reducing the likelihood of developing mental health issues such as anxiety, depression, or post-traumatic stress disorder.

Individuals with higher levels of resilience tend to have a more positive outlook and the ability to bounce back from challenges. This adaptability contributes to better mental health outcomes, lower stress levels, and a more optimistic view of life.

Resilience fosters effective coping mechanisms, problem-solving skills, and a growth mindset, which all play a significant role in maintaining mental health. It enables individuals to confront and manage difficult emotions and situations more effectively, promoting overall mental well-being.

In essence, the presence of resilience can act as a shield against the negative impact of stressors and adversities on mental health, contributing to a more positive and robust emotional state. Strengthening resilience through various strategies and supportive environments plays a vital role in promoting and maintaining mental health.

Resilience is not an inherent trait but a skill that can be developed and strengthened over time. By cultivating a positive mindset, effective coping strategies, problem-solving skills, and maintaining supportive connections, individuals can build resilience and effectively navigate life's challenges. It's the ability to adapt, grow, and emerge stronger from adversities that truly defines resilience.

This exploration has underscored the importance of building resilience in handling life's challenges. By emphasizing the development of a positive mindset, coping strategies, and problem-solving skills, it highlights the role resilience plays in not just overcoming adversity but thriving in the face of it.

CHAPTER SEVEN

Exploring Past Trauma and Its Connection to Present Anger

Trauma, stemming from distressing or disturbing experiences, can significantly impact an individual's emotional and psychological well-being. Its effects often linger, influencing various aspects of a person's life, including their emotional responses, behavior, and relationships. Understanding the link between past trauma and present anger is crucial in addressing and managing these complex emotional responses.

Trauma can manifest in various forms, ranging from physical abuse, emotional neglect, to witnessing disturbing events. It could be a single distressing incident or a series of events causing deep emotional wounds. When traumatic experiences remain unprocessed or unresolved, they can lead to a range of emotional, cognitive, and behavioral difficulties.

Trauma can be a significant contributor to the experience and expression of anger in the present. While not everyone who has experienced trauma becomes angry, for some, trauma can deeply influence their emotional responses, including anger. The manifestation of anger in these individuals can often be a result of unresolved emotions related to past traumatic experiences.

Unresolved trauma can manifest in various ways, one of which is through anger. Individuals who have experienced trauma may express their pain, fear, or hurt through anger, using it as a defense mechanism or a way to cope with overwhelming emotions. The inability to process and heal from the trauma can lead to the mismanagement of emotions, resulting in uncontrolled or intense outbursts of anger.

Trauma-related triggers, which could be anything reminiscent of the traumatic experience, can incite strong emotional responses, including anger. These triggers might be specific situations, environments, or even specific words or actions that subconsciously remind the individual of the past trauma. The response could be immediate, intense, and often disproportionate to the current situation due to the connection it has with past events.

The connection between past trauma and present anger often affects relationships. Individuals may struggle with trust, intimacy, and emotional connections due to their unresolved trauma and resulting anger. Frequent outbursts or emotional distancing can strain relationships, leading to misunderstandings and conflicts.

To manage the pain from past trauma, individuals might develop coping mechanisms that involve using anger as a defense. These may include avoiding situations that trigger memories,

substance abuse, or even becoming overly controlling or aggressive in their interactions. While these behaviors might offer temporary relief, they often exacerbate the issue in the long run.

Addressing past trauma and its connection to present anger involves a journey of healing and recovery. Seeking professional help from therapists, counselors, or support groups specialized in trauma can aid in this process. Techniques such as trauma-focused therapy, cognitive-behavioral interventions, and other evidence-based practices can help individuals process and manage their trauma-related anger.

Creating environments that are sensitive to trauma and its effects is vital for individuals dealing with past trauma and anger. This approach, known as trauma-informed care, involves fostering safe and supportive spaces that acknowledge the impact of trauma. It focuses on empowering individuals and fostering resilience rather than re-traumatizing them.

Recovery from trauma and managing anger is a journey toward empowerment and growth. By addressing the roots of trauma, individuals can learn healthy coping mechanisms, regulate emotions, and rebuild relationships. It's a process that demands patience, self-compassion, and a commitment to change.

Exploring the connection between past trauma and present anger is critical in understanding how unresolved emotional wounds can manifest in current behaviors and emotions. Acknowledging the impact of trauma on anger and seeking appropriate help and support is fundamental in the journey toward healing and recovery. Through trauma-informed care and effective therapeutic interventions, individuals can learn to manage their anger and work towards resolving their past traumas, fostering healthier, more fulfilling lives.

Therapeutic Approaches to Healing Emotional Wounds

Emotional wounds encompass a broad spectrum of experiences, from traumatic events to deep-seated emotional distress caused by various life circumstances. These wounds can result from adverse childhood experiences, relationship issues, grief, loss, or traumatic events, leaving an indelible mark on an individual's emotional and mental state.

Therapeutic approaches are diverse and tailored to suit individual needs, aiming to guide individuals through the process of healing emotional wounds. These methods serve as a structured, supportive framework to navigate and address emotional distress effectively.

Counseling and Psychotherapy

Counseling and psychotherapy offer a safe space for individuals to explore their emotions, experiences, and thoughts in a supportive environment. Therapists employ various modalities, such as cognitive-behavioral therapy (CBT), psychodynamic therapy, or humanistic approaches, to help individuals understand and process their emotional wounds.

Cognitive-Behavioral Therapy (CBT)

CBT focuses on identifying and restructuring negative thought patterns that contribute to emotional distress. It helps individuals understand the connection between thoughts, feelings, and behaviors, aiming to reframe negative thoughts to promote healthier emotions and behaviors.

Psychodynamic Therapy

This therapeutic approach delves into unconscious processes and past experiences, aiming to unearth underlying causes of emotional distress. By exploring past traumas or experiences, psychodynamic therapy aids in resolving emotional wounds and promoting healing.

Humanistic and Person-Centered Therapy

Humanistic approaches, including person-centered therapy, focus on an individual's self-actualization and personal growth. These methods aim to create a supportive and non-judgmental environment, fostering self-awareness and healing emotional wounds by nurturing an individual's inherent strengths.

Trauma-Focused Therapies

Specifically designed for addressing trauma-related wounds, these therapies include Eye Movement Desensitization and Reprocessing (EMDR) and trauma-focused CBT. These methods assist individuals in processing traumatic events and managing associated emotional distress.

Art Therapy and Expressive Arts

Art therapy and expressive arts provide a creative outlet for individuals to express and explore their emotions through various artistic forms. These approaches aid in processing emotional wounds, as the creative process allows for non-verbal expression and exploration of feelings.

Mindfulness-Based Approaches

Mindfulness-based therapies, such as Mindfulness-Based Stress Reduction (MBSR) or Mindfulness-Based Cognitive Therapy (MBCT), focus on present-moment awareness and acceptance. These approaches aid in managing emotional wounds by promoting self-compassion, stress reduction, and emotional regulation.

Family Therapy and Relationship Counseling

Family therapy and relationship counseling address emotional wounds within the context of family dynamics or relationships. These approaches foster better communication, understanding, and resolution of emotional distress within interpersonal relationships.

Support Groups and Peer Counseling

Support groups and peer counseling offer a communal space for individuals to share experiences, offering mutual support and understanding. These platforms provide a sense of belonging and validation, aiding in healing emotional wounds through shared experiences and coping strategies.

Holistic Approaches

Holistic therapeutic approaches, encompassing practices such as yoga, meditation, acupuncture, and mindfulness, focus on addressing emotional wounds by considering the interconnectedness of mind, body, and spirit. These methods aim to promote balance, stress reduction, and emotional healing.

Challenges in Therapeutic Approaches

Navigating emotional wounds through therapy can present challenges. Factors such as resistance to change, fear of vulnerability, or difficulties in trusting the therapeutic process can hinder progress in healing emotional wounds.

Therapeutic approaches play a crucial role in helping individuals address and heal emotional wounds. From diverse modalities like counseling, trauma-focused therapies, art therapy, mindfulness, and family therapy, these methods offer structured and supportive frameworks to process emotional distress effectively. By fostering understanding, processing past traumas, and promoting emotional regulation, these approaches serve as essential tools in the journey toward healing emotional wounds.

Addressing Underlying Issues for Long-Term Anger Management

Long-term anger management involves more than simply controlling anger outbursts in the moment. It requires a deep and holistic approach that seeks to address underlying issues contributing to anger. To effectively manage anger over the long term, individuals must explore the root causes of their anger, work on emotional regulation, and develop healthy coping strategies. This comprehensive exploration delves into the multifaceted aspects of addressing underlying issues for long-term anger management.

Anger is a natural human emotion that serves as a response to perceived threats, injustices, or frustration. It is neither inherently good nor bad, but it becomes problematic when it is expressed in unhealthy or harmful ways. Understanding anger is the first step in addressing underlying issues.

Uncontrolled anger can manifest in various ways, including verbal aggression, physical violence, passive aggression, and internalized anger. Recognizing these signs is essential for addressing the underlying issues contributing to anger problems.

To achieve long-term anger management, it is crucial to explore the root causes of anger. These underlying issues can vary from person to person and may include:

1. Unresolved Trauma: Past traumas, such as physical, emotional, or sexual abuse, can trigger deep-seated anger issues that need to be addressed.

2. Chronic Stress: High levels of stress over extended periods can lead to chronic anger issues. Stress management is essential for long-term anger control.

3. Unmet Needs: Unmet emotional, psychological, or physical needs can result in persistent anger. Identifying and addressing these needs is vital.

4. Inadequate Coping Mechanisms: Inability to cope with life's challenges effectively can lead to anger problems. Developing healthier coping mechanisms is necessary.

5. Communication Problems: Poor communication skills, both in expressing oneself and understanding others, can result in frequent anger episodes.

6. Underlying Mental Health Conditions: Certain mental health conditions, such as depression, anxiety, or personality disorders, can contribute to anger issues.

7. Substance Abuse: Substance abuse can exacerbate anger problems, and addressing the addiction is essential for long-term anger management.

Self-awareness is a critical component of addressing underlying anger issues. It involves recognizing one's emotional triggers, thought patterns, and physiological responses to anger. Self-awareness enables individuals to identify the root causes of their anger and take proactive steps to address them.

Emotional regulation is a key aspect of long-term anger management. It involves learning to recognize and manage one's emotions effectively. Techniques for emotional regulation include:

1. Deep Breathing: Deep breathing exercises help in calming the physiological response to anger.

2. Mindfulness: Practicing mindfulness allows individuals to stay present in the moment, reducing emotional reactivity.

3. Cognitive Restructuring: Identifying and challenging negative thought patterns that contribute to anger.

4. Physical Activity: Regular physical exercise helps in reducing stress and enhancing emotional well-being.

5. Relaxation Techniques: Progressive muscle relaxation, guided imagery, and other relaxation methods promote emotional regulation.

Therapeutic interventions are invaluable in addressing the underlying issues of long-term anger management. Therapists and counselors employ various approaches, such as cognitive-behavioral therapy (CBT), anger management therapy, and trauma-focused therapy, to help individuals explore and resolve their anger issues.

CBT focuses on identifying and changing negative thought patterns and behaviors. It helps individuals understand the connection between thoughts, emotions, and actions, enabling them to manage anger more effectively.

Specialized anger management therapy is designed to address the specific issues that contribute to anger problems. It provides tools and strategies for recognizing triggers and responding to anger in healthier ways.

For individuals with a history of trauma, trauma-focused therapy, such as Eye Movement Desensitization and Reprocessing (EMDR) or prolonged exposure therapy, helps process traumatic experiences and reduce anger-related symptoms.

Participating in group therapy or support groups allows individuals to connect with others facing similar challenges. Sharing experiences and learning from others can be highly beneficial for long-term anger management.

In some cases, medication may be prescribed to address underlying mental health conditions contributing to anger problems. Antidepressants or anti-anxiety medications can help manage anger when used in conjunction with therapy.

Healthy Coping Strategies

Developing healthy coping strategies is essential for long-term anger management. These strategies can include:

1. Problem-Solving Skills: Learning effective problem-solving techniques to address the issues that trigger anger.

2. Effective Communication: Developing strong communication skills aids in expressing emotions and resolving conflicts without resorting to anger.

3. Stress Management: Identifying and managing stress through stress reduction techniques, time management, or relaxation methods.

4. Self-Care Practices: Self-care, including exercise, a balanced diet, adequate sleep, and relaxation, plays a significant role in long-term anger management.

Mindfulness practices and meditation foster emotional regulation by promoting self-awareness and reducing emotional reactivity. These techniques are beneficial for addressing underlying issues contributing to anger problems.

Keeping an anger journal helps individuals track their anger episodes, identifying triggers, thought patterns, and emotional responses. Journaling provides insight into the root causes of anger.

Making lifestyle adjustments is often necessary for long-term anger management. These adjustments may include changing job roles, addressing relationship issues, or finding healthier ways to cope with stress.

In some cases, anger may be rooted in past grudges, resentments, or unresolved conflicts. Forgiveness and the practice of letting go can be transformative in releasing pent-up anger and addressing underlying issues.

Conflict in relationships can be a significant source of anger. Learning conflict resolution skills and addressing relationship issues is vital for long-term anger management.

Long-term anger management is not without challenges. Individuals may face resistance to change, emotional barriers, or difficulties in addressing deep-seated emotional wounds. Overcoming these challenges requires patience, self-compassion, and a commitment to personal growth.

For individuals with severe or deeply rooted anger issues, seeking professional help is essential. Therapy, counseling, and anger management programs can provide the guidance and support necessary for addressing underlying issues and developing long-term anger management strategies.

Long-term anger management requires a holistic approach that addresses underlying issues contributing to anger. Through self-awareness, emotional regulation, therapeutic interventions, healthy coping strategies, and lifestyle adjustments, individuals can effectively manage and resolve their anger issues. It's an ongoing process that involves self-reflection, dedication, and a commitment to personal growth, ultimately leading to a more balanced and fulfilling life.

CHAPTER EIGHT

Creating a Personalized Anger Management Plan

Creating a personalized anger management plan is an essential step towards understanding, addressing, and effectively managing one's anger. This individualized approach involves recognizing personal triggers, developing coping strategies, and implementing techniques tailored to an individual's specific needs. By creating a structured and personalized plan, individuals can navigate their anger issues in a proactive and constructive manner. This comprehensive exploration delves into the elements involved in designing a personalized anger management plan.

The initial step in creating a personalized anger management plan involves self-assessment. This involves identifying personal triggers, situations, or thought patterns that lead to anger. Understanding these triggers may include examining past experiences, stressors, relationship conflicts, or other factors that contribute to anger episodes.

Individuals need to recognize the early signs of anger escalation. These signs may include physiological changes such as increased heart rate or clenched fists, cognitive signs like racing thoughts or irrational thinking, or behavioral signs such as irritability or pacing. Identifying these warning signs helps in implementing proactive measures to prevent full-blown anger outbursts.

An essential component of a personalized anger management plan is the development of coping strategies. These strategies can include various techniques tailored to an individual's needs:

1. Relaxation Techniques: Engaging in relaxation methods such as deep breathing exercises, progressive muscle relaxation, or guided imagery helps in managing stress and calming down during moments of anger.

2. Mindfulness and Meditation: Practices that promote mindfulness and meditation aid in staying present, reducing emotional reactivity, and fostering emotional regulation.

3. Physical Exercise: Regular physical activity helps in releasing built-up tension, reducing stress, and promoting emotional well-being.

4. Healthy Communication Skills: Improving communication skills aids in expressing oneself effectively, reducing misunderstandings, and avoiding conflicts that might lead to anger.

5. Cognitive Restructuring: Recognizing and challenging negative thought patterns that contribute to anger is essential for developing healthier emotional responses.

Maintaining an anger journal is a valuable tool in a personalized anger management plan. Recording anger episodes, triggers, thoughts, and emotional responses provides insight into one's anger patterns. It aids in identifying trends and understanding recurring themes, facilitating targeted interventions.

For some individuals, seeking professional help is an integral part of their personalized anger management plan. Therapists, counselors, or anger management specialists provide guidance and support, helping individuals address deeper underlying issues contributing to their anger.

Lifestyle adjustments can significantly contribute to managing anger. These adjustments might include changes in daily routines, stress management techniques, better sleep habits, or adjustments in work-life balance.

Creating a supportive network is vital in a personalized anger management plan. Seeking support from family, friends, support groups, or other trusted individuals aids in dealing with emotional challenges.

Learning to set boundaries and practicing assertiveness helps individuals communicate their needs and preferences effectively, reducing the likelihood of conflicts that trigger anger.

Engaging in activities that serve as healthy outlets for anger is crucial. These can include art, writing, sports, or other hobbies that provide a constructive way to release emotional tension.

In some cases, anger might be rooted in past grievances or conflicts. Working towards forgiveness and practicing the art of letting go helps in reducing the emotional burden.

The success of a personalized anger management plan depends on personal commitment and consistency. Consistently implementing strategies, learning from setbacks, and persistently applying coping techniques contribute to the efficacy of the plan.

Periodically assessing progress and making necessary adjustments to the plan is essential. Flexibility in making changes based on what works and what doesn't is crucial for long-term success.

Creating a personalized anger management plan involves a comprehensive and tailored approach to address individual triggers, responses, and coping strategies. Through self-assessment, recognizing triggers, developing coping techniques, seeking support, and consistently applying these strategies, individuals can effectively manage their anger. The development of a personalized plan is a dynamic process that evolves over time, requiring dedication, self-reflection, and a commitment to personal growth and emotional well-being.

Overcoming Relapses and Sustaining Progress

Certainly, sustaining progress in anger management involves a continuous effort and resilience, especially when facing relapses or setbacks. Overcoming relapses and maintaining progress is an integral part of the journey towards effectively managing anger in the long term. This comprehensive exploration delves into the strategies and approaches essential in navigating relapses and sustaining progress in anger management.

Relapses, setbacks, or instances of recurring anger episodes are natural occurrences in the process of managing anger. They may be triggered by various stressors, unresolved issues, or circumstances that evoke intense emotions.

Identifying triggers and early warning signs of impending anger episodes is crucial. These triggers may be situational, emotional, or cognitive. Recognizing these warning signs helps in implementing preemptive strategies.

Self-reflection is instrumental in understanding the causes of relapses. Analyzing the circumstances, emotions, and thought patterns leading to a relapse aids in recognizing patterns and making necessary adjustments.

Developing resilience is pivotal in overcoming relapses. Resilience enables individuals to bounce back from setbacks, learn from experiences, and continue their progress in anger management.

Implementing healthy coping strategies during relapses is essential. Techniques such as deep breathing, mindfulness, or physical exercise aid in managing the immediate surge of anger.

During relapses, seeking support from friends, family, or professional help from therapists or counselors is crucial. Support networks offer guidance, encouragement, and additional tools for managing relapses.

Consistency in implementing coping techniques is vital in overcoming relapses. Continually practicing relaxation methods, cognitive restructuring, and mindfulness maintains progress.

Adapting and modifying coping strategies based on the situation is essential. Being flexible allows for the implementation of different techniques depending on the severity of the relapse.

Practicing mindfulness helps in recognizing and acknowledging emotions without reacting impulsively. Emotion regulation techniques aid in managing intense feelings during relapses.

Managing stress plays a critical role in preventing relapses. Stress reduction techniques, time management, and lifestyle adjustments aid in reducing the likelihood of anger episodes.

Improving conflict resolution skills helps in addressing issues that might lead to relapses. Effective communication and negotiation techniques assist in resolving conflicts constructively.

Viewing relapses as learning opportunities is key. Assessing what triggered the relapse and identifying new strategies for managing similar situations in the future is essential for sustained progress.

Having a growth mindset involves seeing relapses as part of the learning process. Embracing the opportunity to learn and grow from setbacks fosters progress in anger management.

In cases where anger is linked to past conflicts or grievances, practicing forgiveness and letting go is crucial. Releasing resentments aids in preventing future relapses.

Having a supportive network is crucial in overcoming relapses and sustaining progress. Seeking support from peers or professionals provides guidance and encouragement.

Maintaining a commitment to personal growth and development is key. Continuously working on self-improvement aids in overcoming relapses and maintaining progress.

Consistency and persistence are essential in overcoming relapses. Persistently applying coping techniques, despite setbacks, is crucial in managing anger.

Periodically assessing progress and making necessary adjustments to the approach is essential. Evaluating what works and what doesn't allows for necessary modifications.

Overcoming relapses and sustaining progress in anger management involves resilience, self-reflection, healthy coping strategies, and a commitment to personal growth. By recognizing triggers, seeking support, and consistently applying coping techniques, individuals can navigate relapses and continue their journey towards effectively managing anger. The process involves embracing setbacks as learning opportunities and making necessary adjustments to the approach for sustained progress in anger management.

Building a Support Network for Continued Growth

Building a support network is a crucial element in the journey of continued growth in anger management. A robust support network provides individuals with the guidance, encouragement, and resources necessary to effectively manage anger over the long term. This comprehensive exploration delves into the strategies and approaches essential in constructing and maintaining a support network for ongoing growth in anger management.

A support network is an invaluable asset in anger management. It offers individuals a safety net, a sounding board, and a source of motivation to navigate challenges and sustain progress. The importance of a support network can't be overstated in the context of anger management.

Types of Support in Anger Management

Support in anger management can come from various sources:

1. Family: Family members often play a pivotal role in providing support, encouragement, and understanding.

2. Friends: Trusted friends can offer a listening ear, perspective, and a sense of camaraderie.

3. Support Groups: Participating in support groups with individuals facing similar challenges provides a sense of belonging and shared experiences.

4. Therapists and Counselors: Professionals in the field of mental health and anger management offer guidance and therapeutic interventions.

5. Online Communities: Online forums and communities provide a virtual space for individuals to connect, share experiences, and seek advice.

6. Self-Help Resources: Books, articles, and self-help resources offer information and strategies for managing anger.

Building a Support Network

Constructing a support network involves several key steps:

1. Identify Your Needs: Start by identifying your specific needs in anger management. What kind of support do you require? What areas of anger management do you struggle with the most? Understanding your needs is the first step in seeking the right support.

2. Reach Out to Family and Friends: Share your goals and challenges with close family members and friends. Their support, understanding, and encouragement are often readily available.

3. Consider Support Groups: Investigate local or online support groups focused on anger management. These groups provide a community of individuals dealing with similar issues and offer a safe space to share experiences.

4. Seek Professional Help: Consult therapists or counselors with expertise in anger management. They can provide tailored guidance, coping strategies, and therapeutic interventions.

5. Online Resources: Explore online communities, forums, and resources dedicated to anger management. These platforms can offer valuable advice, tips, and a sense of connection.

6. Education and Self-Help: Educate yourself about anger management through books, articles, and self-help resources. These materials provide insights and strategies for personal growth.
7. Strengthen Communication Skills: Effective communication is a key aspect of anger management. Consider enrolling in communication courses or workshops to enhance these skills.
8. Participate in Workshops and Seminars: Attend anger management workshops or seminars to gain a deeper understanding of the topic and acquire practical techniques.
9. Networking Events: Attend networking events or conferences related to anger management to connect with experts and individuals on a similar journey.
10. Leverage Technology: Use apps and digital tools designed for anger management, which often include relaxation exercises and anger tracking features.

Developing Supportive Relationships

Building a supportive network involves developing and maintaining relationships with individuals who understand, empathize, and encourage your anger management goals. Key elements in developing supportive relationships include:

1. Effective Communication: Practice open, honest, and effective communication with your support network. Share your feelings, experiences, and challenges, and be open to receiving feedback.
2. Empathy: Seek individuals who display empathy and understanding, as they are more likely to provide meaningful support.
3. Active Listening: Encourage active listening within your support network, where individuals attentively listen and respond to your concerns.
4. Trust: Trust is a foundational element in any support network. Develop trust by being reliable and consistent in your interactions.
5. Mutual Respect: Respect the boundaries, opinions, and feelings of individuals in your support network. Respect is essential for maintaining healthy relationships.
6. Healthy Feedback: Encourage constructive feedback from your support network. Feedback should be honest, respectful, and focused on growth.

7. Reciprocity: Support is a two-way street. Be willing to provide support, listen, and assist others in your network when they require it.
8. Maintaining Boundaries: Establish and maintain boundaries within your relationships to ensure that your support network remains healthy and supportive.

Dealing with Relapses and Setbacks

In the journey of anger management, relapses and setbacks are common. Dealing with these challenges within your support network involves:

1. Honesty: Be honest about your relapses and setbacks. Sharing your experiences with your network can lead to a deeper understanding of your needs.
2. Constructive Feedback: Seek constructive feedback from your support network to gain insights into the causes of relapses and strategies for improvement.
3. Positive Reinforcement: Encourage positive reinforcement within your network. Acknowledge and celebrate the progress you've made, even in the face of setbacks.
4. Adapting Strategies: Be open to adjusting your anger management strategies based on your experiences with relapses. Flexibility is essential for continued growth.
5. Seeking Professional Help: If relapses persist, consider seeking additional professional help from therapists or counselors.

Consistency and Perseverance

Consistency and perseverance are crucial in maintaining a support network for continued growth in anger management. To sustain progress, it's important to:

1. Stay Committed: Maintain a strong commitment to your anger management goals. Consistency in seeking support and practicing coping strategies is essential.
2. Learn from Setbacks: Embrace setbacks as learning opportunities. Analyze the causes and develop strategies to prevent similar relapses in the future.
3. Adapt and Adjust: Be willing to adapt and adjust your anger management approach as needed. Strategies that worked in the past may need modification as circumstances change.
4. Measuring Progress: Periodically assess your progress in anger management. Consider your achievements, areas for improvement, and make necessary adjustments to your approach.

Building a support network is an essential aspect of continued growth in anger management. This network provides individuals with the guidance, understanding, and encouragement needed to navigate challenges, sustain progress, and develop healthy anger management strategies. By identifying needs, seeking support, maintaining healthy relationships, dealing with relapses, and staying consistent in the pursuit of anger management goals, individuals can effectively manage their anger over the long term.